Developing the evidence base for social work and social care practice

Peter Marsh and Mike Fisher

in collaboration with Nigel Mathers and Sheila Fish

First published in Great Britain in November 2005
by the Social Care Institute for Excellence

© SCIE 2005
All rights reserved

ISBN 1-904812-30-9

Written by Professor Peter Marsh and Professor Mike Fisher in collaboration with
Professor Nigel Mathers and Dr Sheila Fish

Produced by The Policy Press
Fourth Floor, Beacon House
Queen's Road
Bristol BS8 1QU
tel 0117 331 4054
fax 0117 331 4093
tpp-info@bristol.ac.uk
www.policypress.org.uk

This report is available in print and online
www.scie.org.uk

Social Care Institute for Excellence
Goldings House
2 Hay's Lane
London SE1 2HB
tel 020 7089 6840
fax 020 7089 6841
textphone 020 7089 6893
www.scie.org.uk

List of abbreviations

AHP	Allied and health professions
BBSRC	Biotechnology and Biological Sciences Research Council
CAM	Complementary and alternative medicine
CCETSW	Central Council for Education and Training in Social Work
CEBSS	Centre for Evidence-based Social Sciences
CSSR	Councils with Social Services Responsibility
DEL	Department of Employment and Learning
DfES	Department for Education and Skills
DH	Department of Health
EPSRC	Engineering and Physical Sciences Research Council
ESRC	Economic and Social Research Council
FHS	Family Health Services
GP	General practitioner
GSCC	General Social Care Council
HEFC	Higher Education Funding Council
HEFCE	Higher Education Funding Council for England
HEFCS	Higher Education Funding Council for Scotland
HEFCW	Higher Education Funding Council for Wales
HRM	Human resources management
JUC-SWEC	Joint University Council's Social Work Education Committee
MRC	Medical Research Council
NCC RDC	National Coordinating Centre for Research Capacity Development
NHS	National Health Service
NICE	National Institute for Clinical Excellence
OECD	Organisation for Economic Co-operation and Development
PSA	Public Service Agreements
PSSC	Personal Social Services Council
PSSRU	Personal Social Services Research Unit
QR	Quality-related Research
R&D	Research and development
RAE	Research Assessment Exercise
RDSU	Research and development support unit
RSES	Research scientist in evidence
SCIE	Social Care Institute for Excellence
SHEFC	Scottish Higher Education Funding Council
SIESWE	Scottish Institute for Excellence in Social Work Education
SWRC	Social Work Research Centre
Topss	Now known as Skills for Care

Summary

Summary of argument

In essence, this report presents a very simple case that:
- modernisation requires a research infrastructure capable of shifting the basis of social care towards evidence-based policy and practice
- the infrastructure should comprise a research workforce, funding and national, strategic priorities
- no such infrastructure exists to support social work and social care.

The report concludes that:
- an agency should be allocated the strategic role and resources to host an inquiry into and to develop, in collaboration with other stakeholders, a research infrastructure to support evidence-based policy and practice in social work and social care.

Overview of the report

Background

The modernisation of social care places a high premium on evidence. At the level of central government, commitment to service reform is increasingly based on evidence about effectiveness rather than on any partisan political agenda. At the level of citizens, acceptance of professional expertise is increasingly tempered by a well-informed critique, supported by improved access to high-quality information. At the level of service providers, accountable, regulated services means ensuring that practice is based on evidence rather than on past practice or current patterns of service.

The value of research

Within the various kinds of evidence required to inform social care (including citizens' views, practitioners' experience, and organisational audit and inspection), that provided by research plays a special role. The best research is specifically designed to be as free as possible from bias in favour of any interest group or policy position, and potentially provides the most secure basis to inform national policy.

The need for research to be managed

In order to be of maximum value, the production of research has to be managed and properly resourced. Research production requires an infrastructure comprising a research workforce, funding and a framework of national, strategic priorities.

In order to explore the proper management and resourcing of research, the report draws a parallel between social care and general practice, and between their underpinning research disciplines of social work and primary care. The research infrastructure for primary care has been thoroughly overhauled following an inquiry in 1997 (known as the *Mant Report*),[16] which provided a system for generating national, strategic priorities and relevant support programmes, including the establishment of the National Coordinating Centre for Research Capacity Development (NCC RCD).

Data on the impact of these reforms are available from the Research Assessment Exercises (RAE) for 1996 and 2001. During this period, the proportion of Departments of General Practice where the majority of research was of national or international excellence (RAE rating '4' or above) rose from 31% to 88%.

No such measures have been taken to improve the research infrastructure that supports social care. The last review of the topic was in England in 1994, and this review was not followed by any measures to develop strategic thinking or resourcing. In comparison with primary care, therefore, research in social work demonstrates much less progress in achieving the kind of research infrastructure that would support excellence.

This is no one's job and so no one is doing it.

While the proportion of Departments of General Practice producing a majority of research of national or international excellence nearly doubled during the period 1996-2001, only one third more Departments of Social Work achieved this improvement. The current position is that 88% of Departments of General Practice, but only 43% of Departments of Social Work produce research of national or international excellence (see Figure 1).

The comparison demonstrates two points: that significantly less research of national and international excellence is being produced to underpin social care, but also that investment in the infrastructure can produce significant changes in the medium term. Recent proposals for an Institute for Health Research and centres of excellence will strengthen the progress towards patient-centred research: social care research needs similar attention and investment.

Why is research from social work the most relevant evidence?

Employing the parallel with primary care, the report distinguishes between scientific research on causes (biological studies in the laboratory, for example), and research on what works in front-line practice (such as in the primary care clinic). Each kind of research has a specific focus and its own priorities. In social care, effective intervention in the front line requires research that derives directly from practice concerns and offers solutions designed and tested to be feasible in practice. While it is critical to

Figure 1: The comparative improvement in RAE rating '4' or above for Social Work and Primary Care 1996 and 2001

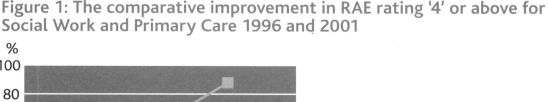

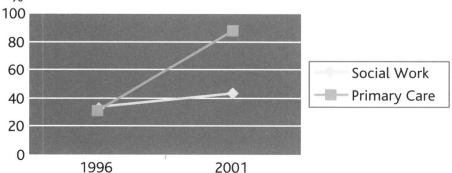

understand the causes of poor parenting or old-age abuse (for example), basic research of this kind does not of itself create an evidence base about effective intervention. As a practice research discipline, social work research (at its best) can do this.

Many research disciplines are also notorious for demarcating narrowly defined aspects of human experience. For example, building an evidence base for social care for children will draw on psychology, education and social policy, but this aspect of social care is not a primary concern of any of these individual disciplines. The best social work research seeks effective interventions to the issues facing social care.

The report further argues that social work research is relevant to the entire range of social work and social care issues. The rigour and relevance of the best social work research should be seen as informing the field of social care as a whole.

Social work research and the relationship with users and carers

The democratisation of welfare, and the move towards citizen participation in social care, requires a different kind of evidence production than one where the professional expertise and the priorities of providers take precedence. As citizens, people who use and provide services need to be directly involved in determining what kind of knowledge should be sought, what research processes should be used and what outcomes matter. The traditions of participatory and empowerment research that permeate the best social work research place it in a strong position to respond to this agenda.

Social work research and the relationship to practice and practitioners

Similarly, the modernisation of social care increasingly requires active collaboration with the social care workforce. Rather than simply seeking to enlighten a workforce portrayed as reluctant to engage in and to use research, more progressive approaches within social work research seek a collaborative partnership with the community of practitioners, identifying their research priorities, how new knowledge can be integrated with existing practice (or can most effectively challenge existing practice), and testing the day-to-day feasibility of interventions.

Most importantly, however, the report identifies the lack of practitioner engagement in research in social care and contrasts this with the promotion of 'lecturer-practitioners' in primary care (and other health professions). The current position is that the more social work researchers engage in research, the more divorced they become from practice: the report argues the need to reverse this arrangement so that practice more strongly informs research.

Resources for research production

Health and social care have different histories and traditions, and this gives rise to striking differences in resources for producing research. The report gives for the first time an account of the resources for social care knowledge production, and draws comparison with those available to support healthcare. The results of this comparison are telling.

On every one of nine different comparators, the disparity in resources is substantial. For example, as a proportion of total annual spend, investment in research and development (R&D) runs at about 0.3% in social care compared with 5.4% in health. The overall annual spend per workforce member stands at about £25 in social care compared with £3,400 in health. Using the more specific comparison with primary care, the annual R&D spend per social worker is about £60, compared with £1,466 per general practitioner (GP); annual university research income from the Higher Education Funding Council (HEFC) Quality-related Research (QR) is £8,650 per social work researcher and £26,343 per primary care researcher (see Figure 2).

Research also requires a research workforce. Again, using primary care as a comparator, social work has about half the number of university-based researchers available to produce research-based knowledge.

Investment in healthcare research is designed to increase the health and competitiveness of the nation, and to reduce inequalities. New proposals for health research promise even greater (albeit targeted) investment. The current disparity between the health and social care research infrastructure reduces the effectiveness of social care in delivering welfare and in reducing inequalities stemming from social factors. In short, the disparity hinders the modernisation of social care.

Figure 2: Selected comparisons between health and social care research and development (R&D) expenditure

2a) R&D budget as a percentage of total

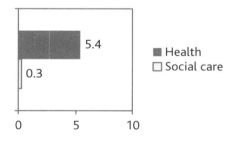

2b) R&D spend per staff member (£)

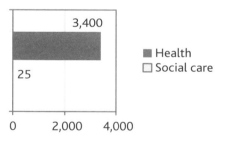

2c) R&D spend per GP and social worker (£)

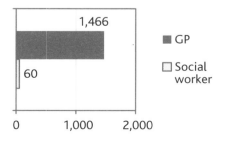

2d) HEFC England QR income per GP and social work researcher (£)

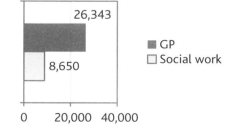

Conclusions

Modernisation provides a unique opportunity to shift the basis of social care towards evidence-based policy and practice. In order to achieve this shift, we need a modern, developed infrastructure for knowledge production producing one of the most valuable kinds of evidence – that from research.

Modern services require an integrated approach between the various agencies providing social and health care, and this in turn calls for each agency to have a well-developed evidence base for its interventions. Put very simply, integrated care will be hindered if social care cannot participate with its sister agencies in basing common policies and practices on evidence.

There are some encouraging signs. The establishment of the Social Care Institute for Excellence (SCIE) and its sister organisations provides a focus for the quality of evidence used to improve policy and practice. Work with the Economic and Social Research Council (ESRC) has provided an opportunity for the first time to obtain greater recognition and investment for social work research. The Joint University Council's Social Work Education Committee (JUC-SWEC) has committed to preparing a national research framework by spring 2006. SCIE is also coordinating work to identify the strengths and weaknesses of UK social work research (in collaboration with the ESRC, JUC-SWEC and the Scottish Institute for Excellence in Social Work Education [SIESWE]). This work, also due in spring 2006, should inform the criteria used in the 2008 RAE to judge the quality of applied and practice-based social work research. In both Scotland and England, reviews of the role of social work provide an important opportunity to examine the resources for knowledge production and the part social workers should play in creating and using the knowledge base.

Recommendations

Policy makers, politicians and the research community have a clear opportunity to make a difference to the quality of the evidence supporting the reform of social care. What is required is to make a start on three key aspects:

- **Review the research infrastructure for social care**. Ultimately, this requires a review paralleling the *Mant Report* for primary care. In preparation for this, SCIE could, in collaboration with its sister organisations, be allocated a medium-term role to coordinate infrastructure development, including identifying some of the key national research priorities and reviewing the options for a national programme of support to develop the social care research workforce. This work would need to recognise the different structures for research and the different agencies developing evidence-based policy and practice in each of the administrations within the UK. It would also need to take account of the development of the new framework for National Health Service (NHS) research.
- **Support the research workforce**. Initially, this might focus on increasing the role of the ESRC in developing the research skills base, so that social care can develop lecturer-practitioners and professional doctorates focusing on practice-based research; Care Councils should also examine their role in increasing the requirement that staff participate in research as part of their re-registration.

- **Develop the resources for research**. Rather than simply arguing for parity of resources with health, the report suggests that resource development should be seen as a long-term process, with an initial focus on maximising investment by ensuring existing programmes of research adequately reflect social work and social care research perspectives and priorities; reviewing the investment in improvement services in order to ensure they are accompanied by research to evaluate their effectiveness; ensuring that commissioners and providers (local authorities, trusts and the independent sector) provide for research funding alongside service provision.

These are some of the measures that can be pursued in the short and medium term to generate the momentum for change towards a research infrastructure that is capable of supporting the modernisation of social care. The case for such change is clear. Doing nothing should not be an option, and the potential benefits for modernisation, and for service users and carers, should be a sufficient spur to action.

1 Introduction

The modernisation of Britain's health and social care services inevitably calls attention to the quality of the knowledge base that can underpin change and development. Research evidence forms a cornerstone of this knowledge base. However, it is pointless to portray evidence in this way unless we have research that gives reliable and valid messages for policy and practice. This is a question of both scope and quality: does the research and development (R&D) agenda yield evidence that is relevant to the core priorities, and is that evidence of sufficient quality to underpin national policy making and to develop practice knowledge?

This report explores the infrastructure for building the knowledge base in social work and social care and in order to do this it draws on some comparisons with primary care. The reasons for this comparison are many. Both are practice-based, front-line services where the relationship with the public (patients, service users and carers) is at the heart of their concerns. They also share a fundamentally similar relationship between practice and knowledge production: social work can appear to be the poor relation of the social sciences in terms of funding and prestige, just as primary care appears to suffer in comparison with the biomedical sciences; both disciplines embrace the need for diverse approaches to generating knowledge (including qualitative research) that leaves them open to the charge of methodological eclecticism; in both cases, everyday practices often lack an explicit evidence base. Perhaps most critically for the purpose of the current report, the infrastructure for primary care research has been a significant focus for analysis and development[1].

The report draws on earlier work based on the Research Assessment Exercise (RAE)[2] and for the first time proposes a method of estimating the investment in R&D in social work and social care in comparison with that made in health care. This comparison is increasingly important as social and health care become more integrated and as social care practitioners attempt to elaborate the knowledge base for their work to their healthcare colleagues. While the term 'social care' describes the welfare sector to which this report applies, we argue that 'social work' is the core research discipline underpinning the knowledge base for policy and practice (there is no academic subject of social care). We therefore describe the infrastructure for 'social work and social care'. Finally, the report argues for better connections between the practice of social work and social care and the R&D community if relevant and useful knowledge is to be produced.

2 The context of modernisation

Concern about the research infrastructure has grown in recent years in parallel with the emphasis on evidence-based practice,[3,4] and this has highlighted the need for 'practice-based evidence'. By practice-based evidence, we mean research directly derived from practice concerns and aimed at providing practice improvement. The policies of modernisation adopted over the past years have also brought an increased emphasis on the evidence base,[5] with some commissioning of research to provide this, but there is also a growing recognition that there is quite simply a lack of relevant and appropriate research that can help to move forward key policy developments: inter-professional practice and learning is one such example.[6] From a central government perspective, policy makers may question whether they can rely on the R&D community to have sufficient engagement with policy to deliver useful and timely evidence,[7] and the Cabinet Office Strategy Unit is increasingly encouraging a more applied approach to generating knowledge, including through the establishment of enhanced capacity for systematic review.[8,9] New proposals from the English Department of Health (DH) for the development of healthcare research give similar priority for research that is relevant to clinical practice.[10]

While there has been little increase in investment in social care research in recent years, there has been serious investment in the dissemination and utilisation of the limited research that is conducted. From early work by the Joseph Rowntree Foundation, with its innovative 'Findings' series, to the pioneering production of research reviews with clear application messages by the DH, there has been a growing knowledge base about the ways that knowledge itself can be disseminated. This has been partnered in more recent years by work on the ways that research can be utilised, as shown in the Social Care Institute for Excellence's (SCIE's) programmes and products, and the activities of 'Research in Practice' and 'Making Research Count'. In Scotland, the Scottish Institute for Excellence in Social Work Education (SIESWE) has provided a focus for research utilisation relevant to education. This substantial dissemination and utilisation work has made the lack of attention to the development of the research products themselves all the more noticeable.

There is of course nothing new in noting the lack of strategic development, particularly in practice-based research.[11] Modernisation and the growing integration of social care with health care has, however, created a pressing need and an important opportunity to change and develop the infrastructure for the production of research knowledge in social care.

3   The nature of evidence and why we need it

So far we have been using 'knowledge' and 'evidence' without detailed definitions, and it is time to clarify the meanings we will attach to these terms and the implications for the focus of this report. Janet Lewis, the former Director of Research at the Joseph Rowntree Foundation, has succinctly captured the role of evidence in the knowledge base for social care in the formula:

> Knowledge = evidence + practice wisdom + service user *and carer* experiences and wishes[12] (italics added)

The importance of this definition is that there is no hierarchy: the three components will vary in importance depending on the question under consideration. Evidence, in this construction, is the product of research, defined as a form of structured enquiry capable of producing generalisable knowledge. The strength of this definition is that research-based knowledge should be of significant value in policy making because it is designed to deliver general messages of wide applicability. However, the capacity of research-based evidence to do this is limited unless we add that evidence deriving from research should be relevant and applied – that is, that it derives from and addresses practice concerns, and is potentially capable of translation into applicable ideas. This gives the formula:

> Evidence = research findings + interpretation of the findings

Using these definitions, the focus of this report is on the infrastructure required to produce evidence from research. We acknowledge that much of what we would define as research is produced within the inspection and audit industry, or from public inquiries (that is, such knowledge derives from structured enquiry and is intended to deliver nationally relevant messages and thus to be generalisable). However, this work is not the subject of this report. We include such knowledge in our definition of research, but its production derives from a quite different infrastructure.

We also need to acknowledge that this report is not primarily about the production of the other two ingredients in Lewis's definition of knowledge – practice wisdom and user and carer experiences and wishes. We will, however, argue that research-based evidence must engage with the interests of practitioners, of users and of carers, and indeed that it must take account of sources that report the experience of providing and receiving services.[13,14] Of course, one way this already happens in producing research-based evidence is through the activities of practitioners, users or carers in leading research.

3.1   Why do we need evidence?

We propose six main arguments for the need for evidence from research within the knowledge base for social care.

First, there is the major impact of the decisions of social care professionals on the immediate life chances of service users and carers (for example, in child protection). In these areas evidence from research can be literally a matter of life or death, and having the best informed practitioners is vital to the immediate outcomes for highly disadvantaged people.

Second, there is the impact over time of decisions on the longer-term life chances of service users and carers (for example, children in care, or long-term carers). Decisions taken over the weeks or months will affect, for example, the educational outcomes for children in care, which are themselves of fundamental importance to their future. To give another example, they will affect the mental and physical health of disabled users and long-term carers, again with substantial implications for their quality of life. Best informed practice should be the right of people whose long-term outcomes depend in part on social care decisions.

Third, good evidence may produce a challenge to fundamental assumptions about social care, and this may bring substantial advantages to service users and carers. When Copernicus developed evidence that the Earth rotates around the Sun, the outcome was not simply a new theory of planetary movement but also the possibility of an entirely different understanding of our place in the universe. On a more relevant and personal scale, research has shown the value of the development of the Expert Patient Programme in healthcare, where people with long-term conditions manage their own care. This programme has the potential to revolutionise the concept of expertise and the relations between providers and patients. Evidence about the effectiveness of family group conferences has the similar potential to change fundamentally the role of the state in protecting children. Research on direct payments has helped to demonstrate the potential to place service users in control of service providers, rather than vice versa. The research has aided these major, and sometimes controversial, shifts in policies, which have the potential to enhance greatly the lives of service users and carers.

The importance of providing safeguards over compulsory or quasi-compulsory decision making is a fourth argument. There are substantial areas of social care where professionals have strong powers, or where the courts may make decisions regarding major aspects of people's lives. Providing the best available evidence is an important component of these processes of control.

Fifth, the evidence is needed for an informed public, who can then engage better with relevant debates about services. Although, at present, there may be relatively few members of the public who actively engage in these debates, it is right that citizens have access to the best evidence.

Sixth, the evidence is needed for informed service user and carer communities, and individuals. Direct involvement in services and engagement with the development of services requires access to the best evidence.

These are six strong arguments for the development of the evidence base, and for shifting social services towards an evidence-based approach, instead of its historic reliance on an 'authority-based' approach.[15] The arguments are remarkably similar to those made for the need for evidence in healthcare (for example, the 1997 report for the DH on *R&D in primary care*).[16] Investment in evidence is clearly of central importance for both social services and health services.

4 Strategic frameworks for developing research

We turn next to some crucial questions in the strategy for knowledge production in social care, and comparable strategies in primary care. How has the production of this evidence been managed in social care? What sort of strategic frameworks have been developed to enhance the applicability of evidence to policy and practice? Are there lessons from the strategic developments in primary care?

A framework for the development of research needs to address four key questions – it should:

* clarify the scope of the field of knowledge to which it applies
* name the questions that need to be addressed if the framework is to progress the strategic development of the knowledge base
* define, in general terms at least, priorities for knowledge production and
* outline the key resource issues over a medium to long-term period to provide this knowledge production.

Ideally, such a framework would be developed by drawing on a thorough analysis of the field, but there have been insuperable difficulties in doing that in social care, because of the scattered and incomplete data available (as we indicate in Appendices 3 and 4 in particular).

At present there is no overarching framework for prioritising or organising the knowledge base in social work and social care. The last major attempt to review R&D in this field was made in 1994 in England, and this report, *A wider strategy for research & development relating to the personal social services*, had little to build on.[17] Indeed, we have to look back to 1980 to find its distant relation – the Report by the Central Council for Education and Training in Social Work (CCETSW) and the Personal Social Services Council (PSSC), on a research strategy for the personal social services.[18] Interim work on the resources for personal social services research,[19] and a review of the research units funded by the DH[20] formed part of the wider picture of policy-related R&D but were not strategically linked. Other DH reports (the 1995 report *Advancing research*[21] and the 1992 *Research capacity strategy*)[22] primarily focused on healthcare and failed to develop any strategic thinking specifically addressed to social work or to social care. The 1994 *Wider strategy* report[17] referred to a pattern of personal social services that has now been so comprehensively superseded that its main interest is simply that it gives historical corroboration to the neglect of the strategic research agenda for social work and social care. This neglect is also evident in the new proposals for National Health Service (NHS) research, which make little reference to social care.[10]

Despite this lack of strategy, social work research has occasionally made a significant impact. For example, the childcare research programme coordinated by the DH in the 1980s produced a degree of coherence on the core questions to be explored and a determined emphasis on relevance to practice (see, for example, two overviews in 1985 and 1991).[23,24] For the first time, we began to see practice-based concepts such as partnership being seriously explored through research. While this example shows how a coherent framework could produce influential, applied, practice-based knowledge, it did not address the question of the infrastructure for research relevant to social care.

It is in one sense hardly surprising that research in social work and social care lacks a strategic framework. No publicly funded body has the task of developing one, no funding agency has the task of promoting it, and the plethora of relevant bodies has not so far offered a unified voice that could command widespread support. Unclear academic roots complicate the process: social work is an academic discipline, and thus receives public funding through the Higher Education Funding Councils (HEFCS), which provides some funding for research in a complex teaching/research distribution to universities, but no major research funder has had the responsibility to fund social work research as an academic discipline. The Economic and Social Research Council (ESRC), the major source of discipline-based, social science research funding,[25] has only recently (2004) recognised social work as a discipline in its own right for the monitoring of research proposals and the provision of research studentships, has now identified it as in need of extra support as an 'emerging' discipline. Social care does not exist as an academic discipline, and while the discipline of social policy has made a significant contribution to the knowledge base (and is recognised by the ESRC), it does not offer a focus on the practice of social care.

Major research units, such as the Personal Social Services Research Unit (PSSRU), and the former Centre for Evidenced-based Social Services (CEBSS), host work that is relevant to social work, but have no publicly funded role to develop it as a research discipline. Indeed, it is arguable that the only major research unit with such a publicly funded role is the Social Work Research Centre (SWRC) at the University of Stirling, whose title derives in part at least from the fact that the term 'social work' is used in Scotland to correspond to what is meant by 'social services' elsewhere.

4.1 The comparison between social care and primary care

The contrast with the history of developing a strategic framework for primary care is telling. As a result of the efforts of the Royal College of General Practitioners and the establishment of academic departments in all UK medical schools, the primary care clinical discipline with the greatest research capacity is general practice. However, in 1995 only 335 out of 31,950 general practitioners (GPs) had academic contracts and many of these were either part time or engaged mainly in teaching. The 1996 Government White Paper *Primary care: Delivering the future*[26] recognised the need to expand the knowledge base for primary care and made the commitment to increase NHS annual funding of R&D related to primary care from £25 million to £50 million. The key turning point, following the commitment to make knowledge production a priority, was the work over some 18 months of the National Working Group on R&D in primary care chaired by Professor David Mant. The publication by the DH in 1997 of the report of this group *R&D in primary care*,[16] which complemented the Medical Research Council's (MRC) previously published topic review *Primary health care*,[27] reaffirmed the importance attached to primary care R&D by the government. This report set out in practical terms a strategy for the expansion of the primary care knowledge base. The overriding strategic objective for the NHS in 1997 was to increase the amount of high-quality R&D of importance to primary care in order to improve the quality and value for money of primary care services to patients.

The report set out guiding principles and specific objectives. The guiding principles were that:

1 High-quality patient care requires a sound evidence base derived from high-quality R&D.
2 High-quality R&D requires effective collaboration between NHS service providers and universities.
3 Any increase in primary care R&D activities in the NHS requires a parallel expansion of R&D capacity in the university sector.
4 Successful expansion of primary care R&D requires a coordinated approach from the NHS, MRC, universities and other funding organisations.
5 Expansion of R&D activities in primary care must build on and preserve existing expertise.

The strategic objectives were:

1 To increase the amount of high-quality R&D of importance to NHS primary care and thus to improve the quality and value for money of primary care services.
2 To increase the recruitment, development and retention of R&D leaders in primary care.
3 To increase the number of clinical staff with R&D expertise.
4 To increase the involvement of staff in non-clinical disciplines (for example, social and behavioural scientists, statisticians and economists).
5 To achieve an evidence-based culture in primary care.

The report set out 23 specific recommendations for the achievement of these objectives. The key recommendations included providing programme funding to support work of strategic importance, establishing young researcher awards to encourage fast tracking of able individuals at an early stage in their careers, establishing career scientist posts for established researchers and developing R&D networking arrangements in each region.

This report was followed up by further work by the R&D Workforce Capacity Development Group[21] and in 2003 by the creation of a National Coordinating Centre for Research Capacity Development (NCC RCD). The ground work for the 2003 development was established in 1996-98 and, as we shall discuss later, in around five years, substantial dividends were seen, for example in the impact on RAE quality indicators (and therefore associated university research funding) and in the establishment of the NCC RCD. This body has recently published its priorities for continuing research capacity development in primary care and it has distinguished three current levels of investment:

1 academic units
2 research and development support units (RDSUs)
3 clinical research networks.

Support is therefore available for both academic staffing and practitioners, with networks and units available for all (some further outline details of the NCC RCD and the personal award schemes are given in Appendix 1).

4.2 Can strategic investment make a difference?

The recognition of the problem in primary care and the strategic investment of resources do appear to have made a substantial difference. Clearly, personal awards are going to encourage practitioners who are conducting research, a point we will return to later, but at the aggregate research level, as shown in national indicators, there are major changes in primary care's substantial research discipline, that of general practice, between 1996 and 2003, and these changes appear directly related to the strategic investment. It should be noted the figures that are available for primary care cover other areas as well (the 'community-based clinical RAE category also has some public health and psychiatric submissions), but the growth that we will outline below was strongly driven by primary care.

The comparison between primary care and social work from 1996 to 2001 is stark.

The 1996 RAE, departments rated '4' or above:

- 7 Departments of General Practice (within the RAE category 'Community-based clinical')[16]
- 11 Departments of Social Work[2]

that is, 31% of the 22 Departments for Primary Care submitted under the RAE and 34 per cent of the 32 Departments of Social Work submitted.

Therefore, before the strategic development and investment in primary care the situation in the two academic areas looked broadly similar. However, the 2001 RAE revealed just how dramatically the situation had changed.

The 2001 RAE, departments rated '4' or above:

- 24 Departments of General Practice (within the RAE category 'Community-based clinical')[28]
- 13 Departments of Social Work[2]

that is, 88% of the 27 returned Departments for Primary Care, and 43% of the 30 returned Departments for Social Work.

Table 1 shows the change over this five-year period.

There was therefore a significant improvement in the RAE ratings, but another way that changes in the strengths of disciplines may be reflected in the RAE process is in the choices made regarding the panel to which work is submitted. If a discipline is strong and has critical mass it will probably submit the great majority of its work to its own discipline panel; if it is weaker, with scattered resources in small units, it is likely to submit under other headings providing greater credibility and scale to other areas. The situation regarding submission levels in the 2001 RAE again indicates the relative strength of the primary care grouping, with increased submission numbers and nearly all of the work going to the relevant discipline panel.

Table 1: Change in percentage of departments rated '4' or above from 1996-2001

RAE year	1996		2001	
Rated '4' or above:	Number	%	Number	%
Primary care	7	31	24	88
Social work	11	34	13	43

RAE submission choices in 2001 were:

• 31 Departments of General Practice; 27 were returned under the relevant panel
• 66 universities had Care Council registered social work programmes; 24 were returned under social work.

The comparison is again stark: nearly all of the primary care group submitted their returns to their academic discipline panel, but under half of the social work group did so.

In passing we might also note a point that we will return to later, which is that it is very difficult to estimate the number of social work departments, units or staff members. In primary care there are reasonably accurate figures for academic staffing; in social work there are next to none.

A strategic approach, with some relevant investment, appears to generate a much broader base of good research. We shall return to these comparisons, and especially to the issue of volume of research, later in the report.

5   Evidence for practice

We have argued so far that there is a clear need for evidence in social work and social care, and that a strategic framework to produce this evidence is lacking. We have made the comparison between social work and primary care, and noted the benefits of a strategic approach and appropriate investment in the latter area. But while there seems little doubt about the need for evidence, and the benefits of suitable planning to produce it, should this evidence for social care come from social work, or from a broad range of disciplines? Our argument here is that a wide range of disciplines can and should play a role in providing the evidence for policy analysis (particularly the discipline of social policy). However, just as primary care requires research from a discipline based in front-line practice, social care for similar reasons requires evidence from social work as the primary discipline rooted in social care practice.

5.1   Why do we need social work evidence?

First and foremost, social care is a practice discipline and, while it requires research from other areas to underpin it, it also requires research based in its own practice for its own development. To discover causes is not necessarily to discover cures, or, to take an example from basic science, what works in the laboratory is not necessarily what works in the clinic. This is fully accepted in health, where, for example, medical research needs to accompany biological research. In a similar fashion, social care needs accompanying social policy research, but it also needs social work research that is practice-based and that will deliver practice change.

Second, all disciplines have their own priorities, based on history, on current fashions, perhaps also on student demand and on international pressures. These priorities may or may not be relevant for social care, but because social work is rooted in social care, it shares the concerns and the pressures of social care practice.

Third, the focus of many disciplines is on discrete aspects of human experience, rather than on the need for an evidence base that addresses the many different issues facing social care. For example, building an evidence base for social care for children and families requires evidence from disciplines such as social policy, psychology and education, but none of these has a primary focus on social care. In contrast, the best social work research integrates knowledge from different disciplines to focus specifically on social care concerns.

Fourth, social work research is relevant to the entire range of social work and social care issues. Its focus is not just on the work of social workers, but on the practice of social care as a whole.

These are substantial reasons to develop social work research in order to improve the practice of social care. Research from social work is not the only relevant discipline, but, at its best, and because of its applied nature and of its relationship with users, carers and practitioners, it is in a position to develop the type of research that will underpin social care practice and service in the future.

In addition, the rigour of the best social work research is an important asset for wider knowledge production in social care. There is an established tradition of good quality research, albeit low in quantity, that provides a sound methodology, within its social science base, for the production of knowledge for social care.

These arguments will lead us to promote strongly the need for a new strategic approach to social work research, and accompanying investment. However, the enhancement of social work research capacity is also relevant to studies undertaken in other disciplines. Evaluations of new programmes, for example, from a discipline base outside social work, will produce more relevant practice knowledge if they are influenced by a strong perspective from social work research. Such a perspective will help to ensure that research focusing primarily on causes also pays attention to cures, and that the practice and implementation activities that need to accompany new programmes are spelled out and well tested. Strong social work research is thus likely to help other research disciplines to improve the relevance of their work to the business of developing practice and policy in social care.

5.1.1   Social work as the core disciplinary base for social care

It is critical to the case for social work research as a core discipline underpinning social care that the subject matter of social work research is not seen as limited to the activities of social workers. To reiterate the points made above, social work skills, knowledge and values are relevant to a wide range of social care activities and deserve study. Of course some activities require higher levels of skilled practice currently requiring (at least) a social work qualification, but we must not confuse 'social work research', with 'research on what social workers do'.

5.1.2 Is social work research distinctive?

We are arguing for the importance of a strong social work research community to assist with knowledge production in social care. This offers, we suggest, a distinctive positive role in the production of relevant evidence. Some would argue it also offers a distinctive role regarding research methods. These debates have been well rehearsed in the papers from the *Theorising Social Work Research Seminar Series* (see papers at www.scie.org.uk/publications/misc/tswr/index.asp), which suggest that social work research methods have distinct qualities, particularly in the way they handle the relationships between individuals, groups and the community. Further distinctiveness is claimed in relation to its attention to participative practices and social justice in the conduct of research itself. The conclusion may be that the strategic framework should use this claim to distinctiveness to elevate the case for investment and recognition.

However, modern forms of knowledge production are increasingly recognised as 'methodologically interdisciplinary',[29] suggesting that the development of methods benefits from less, not more, insularity, and that method distinctiveness is more about emphasis than uniqueness. Moreover, central government customers and commissioners may find the concern with methodological distinctiveness immaterial, in the sense that they commission research that assists policy and practice rather than the development of particular approaches. An important question, therefore, is whether there is value in claiming distinctiveness for social work research methods, when the epistemological tide is running the other way and when this is not the key concern for at least some research users.

Two answers suggest themselves. First, it is important to analyse distinctiveness more closely, and to separate out the argument that social work and social care has its own knowledge base from that concerning the application of knowledge. No modern social science claims exclusive ownership of a knowledge base with fixed boundaries – indeed, it is a mark of a modern discipline that it draws on a wide range of appropriate knowledge. In social work and social care, the core approach is to "place the issue, problem or person at the centre of investigation..." and "to understand events through available knowledge"[30] (see also[31]). The distinctiveness lies not in the knowledge base, but in the application of social science knowledge to social analysis and intervention.

This is most emphatically not to say that social work and social care does not create its own knowledge – the theory and technology of task-centred practice or of family group conferences are sterling examples – but it is to say that it is unhelpful to seek an identity for social work and social care in the creation of exclusive knowledge.

Second, distinctiveness may be far less important in gaining recognition for knowledge production in social work and social care than relevance – that is, the contribution that the knowledge base makes to the understanding of social issues. In this sense, the role that social work has played in revealing child abuse, particularly sexual abuse, and in reducing violence towards children deserves recognition. So too does its work in documenting the effects of poverty, particularly on women, the effects of institutional care, particularly on children, and the effects of social policies that marginalise or exclude people.

Therefore, the argument is to concentrate on distinctiveness in terms of the way social work and social care generates and uses knowledge, rather than on a spurious and rather dated notion of an exclusive knowledge base. We need to concentrate on the focus of knowledge, and the usability of it. Relevance is the hallmark of social work research, not a particular approach to research methodology.

5.1.3 Research *in* or *on* social care? The need for 'relevance squared'

Much of the research evidence for social work and social care practice can only be obtained by research involving practitioners and service users and carers. Resolving the difficult issues that are entailed in this should involve these groups directly. This is an example where social work research can be research *in* social care, rather than research *on* social care. The values of social care need to be central to such involvement, and social work researchers are likely to be best placed to uphold those values. In addition, social work researchers will be well placed to understand the situations that are unique to social work (for example, legal requirements, and models of decision making with families). Social work researchers would be likely to approach the business of research with a set of skills and values relevant to the practitioners, service users and carers they will meet. But while this is a very important element of the arguments for the contribution of social work research, it is not the main one, which, as noted above, hinges around relevance.

Social care knowledge production needs research that can be used in practice. It needs research that begins and ends in practice: that begins with practice-relevant questions, and that ends with relevant material that can be applied in practice.

Relevance needs to be built in both during the design of the research and afterwards when useful ideas are being developed from it. Of course there are 'translation' issues from research studies, but they are significantly reduced if the research has at its heart knowledge and understanding of the practice that it is trying to improve.

There needs to be relevance in topic and relevance for the potential translation into action: thus good social work research will have 'relevance squared' at its heart.

5.2 The research relationship with service users and carers

The experiences, needs and wishes of service users and carers are central to the production of useful and relevant knowledge in social care. Social work research has engaged, quite substantially, with service users and carers, but how should this engagement develop within a new and invigorated focus on social care research knowledge production?

5.2.1 Reshaping the relationship with service users and carers

Knowledge production for social work and social care in the UK rightly has a reputation for rethinking the relationship with service users and carers. At the core of this reshaped relationship is the requirement that knowledge production incorporates attention to users' and carers' definitions of knowledge, process and outcomes. A key question in the development of a strategic framework for social work and social care knowledge is, therefore, the nature of the alliance with service users' and carers' movements.

This work needs to be undertaken at a number of levels. First, the framework needs to recognise that many of those producing knowledge are themselves users or carers, and many are producing evidence of national relevance (in the sense of the product of structured investigation, see above). One way of recognising this knowledge is to review and summarise it, so that its further development may be planned: although several important reviews have been undertaken[32-34], they all have limitations in the range of substantive research addressed or in attention to methodological issues. Work by Carr has identified the common issues from a range of R&D on involving users in service improvement,[35] and this work is now being extended to review the impact of carer involvement. The user group 'Shaping Our Lives' is developing a national user network that will give the user movement greater potential to identify common themes across its member groups (see www.shapingourlives.org.uk).

Second, the ethical issues surrounding knowledge production and user and carer involvement must be addressed, and Butler's work produced as part of the *Theorising Social Work Research Seminar Series* is a good starting point[36] that will now need to be set into the context of the Research Governance Framework (www.dh.gov.uk/ PolicyAndGuidance/ResearchAndDevelopment/). The central principle is to recognise the right of users and carers to be involved in all aspects of the knowledge production process, including setting the priorities for commissioning and standards for the ethical conduct of research.

Third, this principle has important consequences for the way social work and social care uses its resources. Alliances are required with the user and carer movements so that their resources to participate can be improved. Here it will not be enough to rest the case on ethical grounds: if inroads are to be made into areas of knowledge production such as commissioning, and the production of systematic reviews, where service users and carers currently play little part, the case will have to include attention to the methodological necessity of adopting the principles of involvement.[13,37]

6 The engagement with practice and practitioners

This report has argued strongly for the need for an engagement with practice in order to improve effective and useful knowledge production in social care. But what form should that engagement take, and how strong is it at present?

6.1 Practice and research

We have argued that research is one of the key components of best practice, and we have also argued that research that begins and ends in practice that is genuinely 'practice-based evidence' is lacking in social care. However, this problem with the research can be turned, and has been turned by some commentators, into accusations that poor research use by practitioners is a result of their lack of research-mindedness, and of their failure to read, to implement or to produce research (see, for example,[38]). Most of this criticism emanates from a narrow view of evidence-based practice, and it is often underpinned by a simplistic understanding of the way knowledge should apply to practice. Shaw has summed up this problem as follows:

> The assumption of most writers of this persuasion is that utilisation of evaluation findings is a relatively straightforward matter. Where it is a problem, it is typically put down to a breakdown in communication or the self-interested resistance of professionals. To regard theory and practice problems in this way is to relegate 'practice' to the subordinate, the acted-upon...[39: 3]

This unwillingness among some knowledge producers, primarily in the academic sector, to engage with the way practitioners use knowledge in practice, or to build collaborative partnerships with the practice community, stands in sharp contrast to work elsewhere. There is now a powerful body of research, derived from working alongside practitioners, on the nature of the practitioner/research relationship,[40] on how practitioners reason,[41-44] on the knowledge components of professional expertise,[45-47] and on the requirements for constructing knowledge as guidance for practitioners.[48] All but one of the researchers quoted in this paragraph work outside the UK, suggesting that the UK academic community has something to learn from its international colleagues about engaging with practitioners.

Given the focus of this report on the research workforce, what does it mean for researchers to be engaged with practice? Rather than suggest some absolute view of this engagement (as, for example, providing direct services), it is more useful to consider a 'gradient' of nearness to practice.

At one end of such a gradient, all researchers with a social work qualification will have an understanding of practice derived from their professional education and training. Senior managers, and senior social work academics, will fall into this group, and they probably are the farthest from practice of all those engaged with social work research. A more substantial group, comprising team leaders and lecturers, will be somewhat closer to practice. They will observe practice, talk to practitioners, and consider, sometimes in great detail, the elements of practice. They will meet service users and carers, but perhaps not all that often, for their engagement with practice is somewhat second-hand. It is the largest group, the practitioners, those directly responsible for services, who are, of course, closest to practice.

Figure 1 summarises these three groups with a suggestion of the relative size of each in the workforce, from the small group of senior staff to the much larger group of practice staff.

It has been argued earlier that the distinctive nature of social work research is the opportunity it creates for the research focus to be relevant to practice and the research to have a high potential for translation into practice. Therefore, we would ideally want the engagement with research production to rise as the closeness to practice rises. In social care the picture is precisely the opposite of this.

The nearer you are to practice the less likely you are to engage with the research production process.

Figure 1 shows that social work research is not making the most of its practice base. Closeness to practice is a major strength that is not being fully used in social work at present.

Figure 1: 'Nearness to practice' and engagement with the research production process

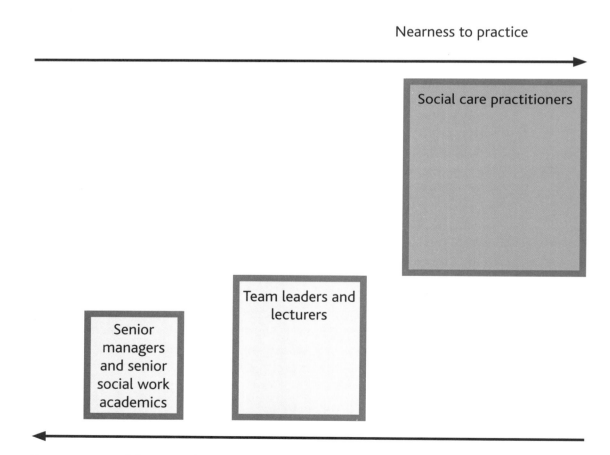

Nearness to practice

Social care practitioners

Team leaders and lecturers

Senior managers and senior social work academics

Engagement with research production

The contrast with primary care is dramatic. The Society for Academic Primary Care states quite clearly that:

> Direct clinical experience is important for academic general practitioners. Apart from its intrinsic benefits for patient care, it provides a source of ideas for both teaching and research, and evidence of credibility with full time colleagues.[28:30]

Senior academic staff with responsibility for research are close to practice because they are in practice. The influence of practice on research is thus direct and clear in primary care. Social work research can, and should, do better to integrate practice with research production.

6.2 Encouraging the engagement between practice and research production

Having a substantial number of practitioners directly engaged in high-quality research work should certainly be one of the longer-term aims if we are to improve the knowledge base of social care. However, there is a model, which occurs in both social work and primary care, of engagement via lecturer-practitioners that could be enacted quite quickly, and which would provide a good, if not ideal, improvement for bringing practice closer research.

The lecturer-practitioner concept has been developed to combine professional activity in both the academic and practice components of the discipline by integrating theory, practice and the teaching of practice.[49] This role is both highly skilled and crucial to the development of a discipline. Such individuals can enter into the academy, challenge and encourage the relevance of research, and assist with its implementation. Some staff in these posts may also receive training to undertake research, beginning to build the skilled practitioner-researcher community that is needed in the longer term. The importance of the lecturer-practitioner's role is acknowledged publicly in current healthcare policy,[50] which states its intention to enhance the status of those who provide practice-based teaching. While research has been undertaken primarily in relation to the lecturer-practitioner role in nursing (see, for example,[51] there have, until recently, been no cross-professional studies of lecturer-practitioners. Studies so far have been within the different professions including engineering, medicine and management,[52] pharmacy, nursing and teacher education[53], as well as healthcare, teaching, law, theology and social work.[54] The move to interprofessional working creates further opportunities, while also adding some new challenges, for the lecturer-practitioner role.[55] All of these studies have investigated access and recruitment, initial professional education, assessment, approaches to teaching and learning and the interconnections between academic culture and the nature of disciplines.

Evidence from these studies, from experience in higher education and more recently the RDSUs based in trusts (for example, Trent RDSU), is that there is substantial pent-up demand from social services practitioners for engagement in research production, and that providing for this demand will produce a beneficial involvement of practice within the academy. The problem is not the lack of good quality staff, nor their ambitions, but rather the absence of opportunity and the funding to accompany it. The ESRC may well be one of the keys to providing funding for the development of practitioner-lecturers, if it could be persuaded, given its current interest in social work, to provide better and more appropriate funding for the post-graduate work, fellowships and so on that would be needed.

6.3 Resources for research production*

The argument so far has been that there is significant need for social work research, that the nature of social work research resides in its relevance to policy and practice, and that there is substantial value in, and substantial need for, a strategic approach to developing social work research. We will now turn to the crucial question of the level of resources that should be devoted to such development, drawing on comparisons with the NHS, in general, and primary care, in particular.

Social work and social care is a major UK enterprise, with around £12 billion expenditure, a workforce of over one million (larger than the UK engineering workforce and in total rather greater than that of the NHS), and serving an estimated one million people each year (it serves 750,000 people each year in England alone). It plays a key role in fostering social coherence and represents a major commitment to a socially just society. What level of R&D funding is appropriate to underpin an enterprise of this size and importance?

6.3.1 Health and social services expenditure and staffing

In common with our arguments earlier, we will approach this question through a comparison with health. There are important qualifications to be made, especially when we turn to research expenditure, but the NHS and the social care sector have some substantial similarities in both their importance to the public, and the resources, both financial and human, that they deploy.

The overall service expenditures and the staffing levels are given in Tables 2 and 3. The figures generally relate to 2003-04, and full details of them, as for all of the figures in this section of the report, are given in the appendices. The staffing figures given here do not show the enormous differences in qualifications and skills between the NHS and the social care sector, but they do indicate the broad comparability of the two endeavours in total staff counts, and the difference in overall expenditure of around 8: 1. As we have shown earlier in the report, however, the ratio of practitioners to research staff is very different: using the comparison between primary care and social work, the latter has approximately twice as many practitioners, but half as many research staff.

Table 2: Service expenditure

	Health	Social services
England	£ 69,369,000,000	£ 10,643,000,000
Wales	£ 4,325,083,000	£ 244,755,000
Scotland	£ 7,775,660,000	£ 230,439,000
Northern Ireland	£ 2,139,800,000	£ 712,600,000
Total	**£ 83,609,543,000**	**£ 11,830,794,000**

---

* Details of sources and figures are in the appendices.

Table 3: Staffing total

Total	Health	Social services
England	1,071,462	1,240,000
Wales	68,472	70,000
Scotland	129,275	112,500
Northern Ireland	39,024	30,000
Total (whole time equivalents for 2003)	**1,308,233**	**1,452,500**
GPs/Social Workers	General practitioners	Social workers
England	29,777	76,300
Wales	1,780	2,768
Scotland	3,921	7,000
Northern Ireland	1,002	1,939
Total	**36,480**	**88,007**
Academic staffing	Community-based clinical	Social Work
Total	**1,177**	**383**

In the appendices we have given full details of the ways in which the figures were obtained. It is important to note the extreme difficulty in obtaining some of the data for social care. It is a major research endeavour in its own right to find nearly all of the information, and some, for example that on academic staff, is simply unavailable. Again, we are faced with the fact that very basic elements of the research infrastructure for social care are lacking in comparison with health.

6.3.2 Health and social care R&D

What level of research investment is available to the health and to the social care sector? We need first to note several issues that affect how we have constructed the following comparisons. The picture is complicated in England by the major structural shift of responsibility for services to children from the DH to the Department for Education and Skills (DfES). In time, this shift will affect research funding, but, as this is not yet clear, the following analysis relies on figures for England from the DH. Since other authors have also noted a relative lack of investment in education research (compared with OECD (Organisation for Economic Co-operation and Development) countries rather than with health expenditure),[56] it will be important as part of the wider inquiry that we propose to explore a three-way comparison between health, social care and education R&D investment.

A second introductory point is that, in any comparison, there is no direct equivalent of the major investment by the pharmaceutical industry in health research, estimated at around £2 billion (1998 figures, estimated by the pharmaceutical industry: note that the Consultative Paper on NHS Research now suggests the total is around £5 billion).[10] In Tables 2 and 3, we show the figures both with and without this investment. Alongside this major finance base there is a substantial investment from others, involving an NHS levy yielding around £450 million annually, accompanied by funding from the DH of around £540 million, MRC spending of around £360 million, medical charities of around £540 million, and the HEFC providing around £233 million. Details are given in Table 4.

Table 4: R&D expenditure

Overall	Health	Social services
Pharmaceutical	£ 2,375,000,000	
NHS levy	£ 442,450,561	
DH	£ 534,700,000	£ 5,300,000
Research Council	£ 359,900,000	£ 2,024,460
Charity	£ 540,000,000	£ 10,650,730
HEFC	£ 233,085,666	£ 18,944,125
Total	**£ 4,485,136,227**	**£ 36,919,315**
Government and Charity	**Health**	**Social services**
Pharmaceutical		
NHS levy	£ 442,450,561	
DH	£ 534,700,000	£ 5,300,000
Research Council	£ 359,900,000	£ 2,024,460
Charity	£ 540,000,000	£ 10,650,730
HEFC	£ 233,085,666	£ 18,944,125
Total	**£ 2,110,136,227**	**£ 36,919,315**
Government direct	**Health**	**Social services**
Pharmaceutical		
NHS levy		
DH	£ 534,700,000	£ 5,300,000
Research Council		
Charity		
HEFC		
Total	**£ 534,700,000**	**£ 5,300,000**
	Primary care	
DH	£ 53,470,000	
University (QR) expenditure		
HEFC England QR Funding (2003-04)	**Health**	**Social work/social policy**
Clinical laboratory sciences	£ 39,624,486	
Community-based clinical	£ 31,005,876	
Hospital-based clinical	£ 90,417,791	
Nursing	£ 5,477,048	
Professions allied to medicine	£ 18,557,179	
Social policy		£ 11,893,613
Social work		£ 3,313,262
Total	**£ 185,082,380**	**£ 15,206,875**

Note: QR = Quality-related Research; HEFCE = Higher Education Funding Council for England.

In an exact parallel of the problems with the workforce data, spending on social work and social care R&D is substantially more difficult to estimate and to allocate to specific countries of the UK. For example, in England, DH funding of specific research units relevant to social work and social care amounts to some £18 million; the major charities have programmes worth some £10 million, and HEFCE funding in social work and social policy amounts to £18 million. Although English Councils with Social Services Responsibility (CSSRs) will be funding some very small-scale research work on low budgets,[57] the absence of a funding stream from them is a remarkable gap.

The role of the research councils is important, despite the relatively light focus on social work that we have already identified. The ESRC, which spent £67 million on social science research in 2003-04, should play a key role in increasing the attention to this sector, especially given its current interest in social work as an 'emerging' research discipline. A recent report by the Joint University Council Social Work Education Committee (JUC-SWEC) showed that, up until 2004, the ESRC had little knowledge of social work as a discipline, and social work was not represented in its structures.[25] The report attempted to identify work of relevance to social work (the ESRC did not, at the time of the research, record social work as a discipline). The authors examined 2,538 successful bids (the ESRC funds around 600 per year) and estimated some 0.6% (15) included a link with social work. A further 32 (1.3%) had an obvious link with social welfare, and a further 22 (0.9%) had a possible link with social work. The total spent on social work and social care by the ESRC is likely to be around £2 million. To its credit, the ESRC is aware of this neglect of social work, as we have noted, and it has agreed to fund, jointly with SCIE, SIESWE and JUC-SWEC, an audit of social work as a research discipline.

Finally, under university funding, in order to maintain the wider health comparison, we have included all of the five discipline headings in health and not taken primary care alone. We have therefore added social policy expenditure along with social work. However, later tables revert to the closer comparison, focusing on social work and primary care (with primary care covered by the *Community-based clinical* heading).

6.3.3 Summary of expenditure and staffing levels

Table 5 shows comparisons in summary forms, with the 'Government and Charity' headings covering all non-pharmaceutical expenditure.

Table 5, therefore, provides the basic data for a comparison of expenditure levels according to different funding sources, related to workforce figures and to service expenditure figures.

6.3.4 Comparing health and social care research investment

Based on the figures in Table 5 we have examined nine comparative areas, and laid out the results, including the ratio of expenditure between health and its social care sibling, in Table 6.

Table 5: Summary totals

R&D expenditure		
Overall	Health	Social services
	£ 4,485,136,227	£ 36,919,315
Government and charity	Health	Social services
	£ 2,110,136,227	£ 36,919,315
Government direct	Health	Social services
	£ 534,700,000	£ 5,300,000
	Primary care	
	£ 53,470,000	
University (QR) expenditure		
HEFCE QR funding (2003-04)	Health	Social work/policy
	£ 185,082,380	£ 15,206,875
	Community-based clinical	Social work
	£ 31,005,876	£ 3,313,262
Service expenditure		
	Health	Social services
	£ 83,609,543,000	£ 11,830,794,000
Staffing		
Total	Health	Social services
	1,308,233	1,452,500
GPs/social workers	GPs	Social workers
	36,480	88,007
Academic staffing	Community-based clinical	Social work
	1,177 (returned staff in RAE 2001)	383

1 Overall R&D expenditure as % of total service expenditure

Nearly all organisations base their thinking about R&D expenditure on their overall expenditure. The opening comparison does this, but there is a key issue of 'like versus like' because of the inclusion of the major pharmaceutical budget in the health research expenditure. Therefore the next comparison removes this element.

2 Government and charity R&D (R&D minus pharmaceutical) as % of total service expenditure

This is a better overall comparative measure given the substantial pharmaceutical funding which is difficult to compare with social care (although the argument could be made that pharmaceuticals are an intervention like any other, and therefore, for example, research expenditure by private care homes, a negligible sum, is one form of equivalent in social care, thus allowing the overall R&D comparison in number 1 above to stand).

3 Government direct R&D (direct central government spend on research) as % of total service expenditure

While we recognise that there should be substantial expenditure from local authorities and CSSRs, there is merit in comparing the expenditure which the government chooses to make on health and on social care (that is, the expenditure from comparison number 2 above minus the charity figures).

There is a stark difference in the figures: the expenditure on health being 16 times that of social care.

4 Overall R&D per head (total staffing

While we fully recognise the substantial differences in the workforce qualification and skill levels in the two different sectors, it is instructive to consider the amount spent per staff member. It provides a crude measure of the research 'product' available to each staff member, and shows a massive disparity. It is again perhaps best examined without the pharmaceutical spending in comparison number 5 below.

5 Government and charity R&D (R&D minus pharmaceutical) per head (total staffing)

This comparison shows the 'research product' available to each staff member in the different sectors, allowing a generous reduction in the health expenditure by removing the pharmaceutical spend.

The expenditure on health is over 60 times that of social care: a major disparity in funding.

But it may be even more worrying that removing the charity element, and just leaving the direct expenditure from government as the comparison (in number 6 below) does not reduce this disparity at all but nearly doubles it.

6 Government direct R&D (direct central government spend on research) per head (total staffing)

This is the direct spend on research from government, to provide 'research product' per head.

There will be some small addition to the social care spend from the (very small) contribution made by local authorities and CSSRs for research, but the headline figure here shows over one hundred times more direct spend by government per staff head in health as compared with social care.

7 Government primary/social care R&D expenditure per GP/social worker

We have argued earlier that research must support people taking crucial decisions about assessment and monitoring of care. In the two areas we are comparing this will centrally involve a comparison of social workers and GPs.

In the comparative figures we have developed under 1-6 above, the better measure of expenditure is probably the one featuring resources directly under government control: therefore we have compared this for the two professional groups. This comparison shows the government research spend per GP and per social worker.

The expenditure for a GP is around 24 times as much as that for a social worker.

8 HEFCE QR as % of service expenditure

The difference in RAE scores between primary care and social work is in substantial part likely to be due to the strategic approach to research development in primary care. This difference in RAE scores in turn leads to funding implications because a research funding component of university income (QR) is based on the RAE score.

This comparison takes the funding made available to universities for research funding under QR, and then compares it with service expenditure.

The university funding councils are under no obligation to match their research spending to the areas most likely to apply to them; nonetheless, it is instructive that the health research funding, if related to service expenditure, is 1.7 times that for social care (taking both social policy and social work funding, the former is more substantially funded per academic than the latter).

9 HEFCE QR per head (academic community-based clinical and social work)

This comparison notes that each academic in primary care generates for the university £17,693 more funding than a social work colleague, substantially due to the RAE scores themselves, which are in turn substantially related to the strategic approach to research development in primary care.

The nine comparisons are outlined in Table 6 below. Whichever measure is used, primary care and health research are always substantially better funded than social care.

The spending on social work as the key research discipline underpinning social care is so far below that in healthcare that it is difficult to see how they can share the same commitment to evidence-based policy and practice. The RAE is not delivering improved funding; indeed, the situation is getting worse. Despite the welcome increased interest by the ESRC, the figures here show the situation is very serious indeed.

The level of resources devoted to relevant and applicable social care research is well below sensible levels for a workforce of this size, for service expenditures at this level, and for the importance of the service to millions of service users and carers.

Table 6: Nine key measures of R&D expenditure

1. Overall R&D expenditure as % of total service expenditure	Health	Social services	Ratio: 1
	5.36%	0.31%	17.29
2. Government and charity R&D as % of total service expenditure	Health	Social services	
	2.52%	0.31%	8.13
3. Government direct R&D as % of total service expenditure	Health	Social services	
	0.64%	0.04%	16.25
4. Overall R&D per head (total staffing)	Health	Social services	
	£ 3,428.39	£ 25.42	134.87
5. Government and charity R&D per head (total staffing)	Health	Social services	
	£ 1,612.97	£ 25.42	63.45
6. Government direct R&D per head (total staffing)	Health	Social services	
	£ 408.72	£ 3.65	111.98
7. Government primary/social care R&D expenditures per GPs and social workers	GPs	Social workers	
	£ 1,465.73	£ 60.22	24.34
8. HEFCE QR as % of service expenditure	Health	Social services	
	0.22%	0.13%	1.69
9. HEFCE QR per head (academic community based clinical and social work)	Community-based clinical	Social work	
	£ 26,343.14	£ 8,650.81	3.05

7 Conclusions

Politicians, policy makers and the public rightly call for better knowledge to underpin the modernisation of welfare. Resources cannot be targeted or used wisely without better knowledge of which services are effective in meeting the requirements of people in need. Nor can the different services work effectively together unless they share a commitment to evidence-informed practice, so that each branch of health and welfare can work from a shared understanding of how to create better outcomes for people.

Although not the only source of knowledge, research plays a key part in generating the evidence base, and this report has noted the signs of progress on this issue in establishing SCIE and its sister organisation in Scotland, in the ESRC's readiness to engage with social work research, and in the support by the Cabinet Office Strategy Unit for a more applied approach to generating knowledge and for the development of systematic review capacity.

However, the report has also demonstrated the stark inadequacy of the current arrangements for producing research-based knowledge to underpin the modernisation of social care.

We have shown that social care lacks the mechanisms and the data to generate the kind of strategic priorities and research infrastructure that the Mant Report created for primary care, which is a close comparator in healthcare. As a proportion of total service spend, investment in R&D runs at about 0.3% compared with 5.4% in health, with no comparable strategic direction at the national or local levels. Again using primary care as a comparator, social work has about half the number of university-based researchers available to produce research-based knowledge. There is no centrally coordinated information on the R&D infrastructure (to the point where on occasion it is difficult to locate even basic information on spending and on the workforce). In comparison with primary care, the RAE is neither driving up standards nor improving resources for social work research. The ESRC does not have a strategic role in developing practice-based or applied research relevant to social care, and there is no single authoritative body speaking for social work and social care research.

Development of the weak research infrastructure in social care is no one's job, and so no one is doing it.

Clearly, the first priority is to generate recognition among policy makers and politicians that the modernisation of social care cannot succeed without an infrastructure for creating the knowledge base. We suggest that the experience of primary care shows a way forward. What is required is an inquiry in social work and social care research, equivalent to the Mant Report,[16] that would produce a blueprint for development, and propose the structural capacity to deliver relevant changes. Such an inquiry should have a UK-wide remit in recognition that knowledge production is a national issue, but it should also take account of the different structures for research and the different lead agencies in each of the administrations within the UK. We suggest the proposed inquiry should focus on four key aspects: resources, priorities for knowledge production, research workforce development and data infrastructure.

7.1 Resources

The disparity between R&D expenditure in health and social care is clearly substantial and demonstrates the weakness of current arrangements to support a research infrastructure for social care. Rather than simply arguing for parity of resources with health, this report suggests that an inquiry should regard resource development as a long-term process with an initial focus on how existing funding can be better employed. Several possibilities may be explored. First, effective social welfare demands an interplay of health and other services, so that existing research in health, education, social policy and criminal justice is likely to deliver less value for money if it fails to address the social care element. It might be necessary therefore to examine how existing research programmes and teams could be made more effective by including social work and social care research dimensions.

Second, the research councils clearly have a key role in generating research that is relevant to a £14 billion per annum social care sector, serving over one million people each year. Currently, the ESRC is collaborating with SCIE, JUC-SWEC and SIESWE in a study of social work research capacity, with a view to agreeing a framework for understanding quality. In view of its importance in improving services, applied practice-based research should be a particular focus for this work, with the aim of increasing both its quality and quantity.

Other research councils may also play a role, where individual research programmes may impact on social care, or where joint work between councils has obvious relevance to social care. A clear example of the latter is the programme on the 'New Dynamics of Ageing' announced by the ESRC, Engineering and Physical Sciences Research Council (EPSRC), Biotechnology and Biological Sciences Research Council (BBSRC) and MRC. This programme of research focuses on one of the key service user groups in social care and it will need to ensure its relevance to this sector (on which it has made a start by requiring academic proposers of collaborative projects to name an 'end-user' as a partner).

Third, central government will need to consider its role in generating the evidence for evidence-based policy and practice in social care, and what level of central funding is appropriate. This should include an examination of the substantial funds dedicated to service improvement (for example, in the Care Services Improvement Partnership established by the English DH) and whether such improvement initiatives should be accompanied by research. Given that in England there are two departments (DH and DfES) with key responsibilities for social services, it is important that social work research is not considered in the separate compartments of children and adults, when there is often overlap and when coherence would be the sensible cost-effective approach. The inquiry proposed by this report must take account of shared responsibilities between different departments in England.

However, resource provision cannot be viewed solely as the responsibility of central government. Those who provide and who commission services should ensure that research is an integral element. Research should be seen as 'core business', not as an optional extra. The inquiry will need to consider how local authorities, CSSRs and trusts can be encouraged to ensure that research funding is provided alongside service provision, and how the RDSUs can play a more substantial role in social care.

7.2 Priorities for knowledge production

The national institutes of excellence in health (NICE) and in social care (SCIE and its sister organisation in Scotland) provide the opportunity to identify gaps in the knowledge base and to underline the need for relevant, applied research. The inquiry should therefore work alongside the relevant institutes for excellence to generate national, strategic priorities that should govern investment. Appendix 5 sets out some current agendas, but these will need to be supplemented through dialogue with a wide range of stakeholders, including central government, the ESRC, the academic community, practitioner, user and carer communities and local authorities, CSSRs and trusts. If research is to be relevant to service improvement, we have argued that practice concerns must drive it, and the inquiry will need to take special steps to create a durable voice for practice in all of its work.

7.3 Research workforce development

Social work and social care does not have enough people engaged in knowledge production. In primary care, the NCC RCD plays a key role in developing the research workforce (see Appendix 1), and the inquiry should consider how a similar development role could be undertaken in social work and social care research. This work would differ from that undertaken, for example in England, by the Strategic Learning and Research Committee[58] in that it would have a primary focus on social care and on solutions that derive from the structures and needs of social work and social care research (rather than from those of healthcare). Research workforce capacity development would need to consider the range of qualifications required, award schemes that are appropriate to the social work and social care workforce, and the links with professional qualifying training and continuous professional development. We have drawn particular attention to the value of the lecturer-practitioner role in primary care, and the inquiry would need to consider how to promote a similar role in social work and social care.

The capacity to produce knowledge is related to, but different from, that required to use research-based knowledge, and a further strand of workforce capacity development will need to concern ways of making research literacy an integral part of professional education and training.

7.4 Data infrastructure

In preparing this report, it was frequently clear that data that were centrally collated for healthcare were not available for social care or were available only by piecing together information from disparate sources. Anyone seeking to monitor the volume of research on social work and social care, the numbers and characteristics of people involved as researchers or as research students, the expenditure on research, or the coverage of topic areas will be defeated unless the inquiry establishes systems to record this kind of data, including a social care research register.

7.5 Next steps

Clearly, this report argues for a thorough Inquiry and that will take time. The Mant Report took 18 months to produce and the establishment of the NCC RCD a further five years. What progress can be made in the interim? We suggest that there are five specific areas where either progress is already underway or a start could and should be made.

First, it is vital that an authoritative body takes the lead in reviewing and providing ideas for developing the research infrastructure in social care. This role fits most naturally with the remit of SCIE, which is, after all, an organisation specifically established to develop service improvement on the basis of evidence, including research-based knowledge. In the future, SCIE will need to develop partnerships with the lead agencies developing evidence-based policy and practice in Scotland. SCIE and its sister organisations are in a unique position to identify the gaps in the knowledge base and the weaknesses in the infrastructure. In collaboration with SIESWE, SCIE has started work on the lack of outcomes-based research and on the role of the ESRC. SCIE is also initiating work to increase systematic review capacity. The DH in England has recently asked SCIE to establish a register of social care research. SCIE also works alongside its sister institute of excellence in health, NICE, and other agencies to press the case for more applied research that is directly relevant to the work it is asked to undertake. In several ways, therefore, SCIE is already acting as stimulus to infrastructure development, and this work could be formalised and focused in a strategic programme. An early step would be to ask SCIE to explore the case for a NCC RCD for research in social work and social care.

Second, there is a greater role for the ESRC concerning the academic skills base. It has already agreed to monitor proposals made under the rubric of social work research, and now has postgraduate training requirements specifically designed for social work as a research discipline. In collaboration with SCIE, SIESWE and JUC-SWEC, the ESRC is co-funding a review that will establish a quality framework for practice-based and applied research: the next step will be for the ESRC to review the way that it can aid the development of skilled researchers in ways appropriate to social care, for example by provision of support for lecturer-practitioners and professional doctorates.

Third, the lack of data on the infrastructure requires leadership from central governments to establish the core monitoring systems to record central and local R&D expenditure. An inquiry would require such data in any case and only central government has the power to require returns from local providers and commissioners on R&D expenditure. Given that some expenditure will be made by trusts, central government could also offer leadership in asking Trusts to support social work and social care research through its RDSUs. It should emphasise the importance of research as 'core business' for the trusts.

Fourth, the Care Councils (that register social care staff and regulate training) and the Sector Skills Councils (that promote workforce development for the social care sector) both have a critical role in developing the research workforce, a role that could be more actively focused on the production and use of research. For example, everyone registered by the Care Councils will need to satisfy re-registration requirements in order to remain on the register: since staff are required by the Councils' codes of conduct to 'maintain and improve their knowledge and skills', it would be perfectly possible to insist that engagement with knowledge production form an essential part of the evidence presented for re-registration. This would have the advantage that employers would need to demonstrate how they have provided opportunities – and resources – to make this possible. The area of post-qualification work is also central, with the urgent need for a research route to advanced qualifications, planned in conjunction with the JUC-SWEC and in liaison with ESRC. The current review of the future of social work in Scotland and the recently announced review in England provide an opportunity to examine resources for knowledge production, and the contribution social workers can make, particularly through the development of career pathways corresponding to the concept of the lecturer-practitioner.

Finally – and in some ways most importantly – the social work research community itself must show active leadership in setting the agenda for infrastructure development and determination in responding to initiatives by others such as the ESRC. Already, the JUC-SWEC has started work on a UK-wide strategic framework for research that will identify priorities, and appropriate training and governance. The work on a quality framework that includes applied and practice-based research, undertaken under the auspices of the JUC-SWEC Research Committee, must then be pursued vigorously in the RAE so that its judgements on quality support the kind of research that is designed directly to address evidence-based policy and practice. What is critical is that the social work academic community maintains its drive and cohesiveness so that there is an authoritative voice for social work research.

These are some of the measures that can be pursued in the short term to generate the momentum for change towards a research infrastructure that is capable of supporting the modernisation of social care. In the longer term a major inquiry needs to chart the way forward.

The case for change is clear. Doing nothing should not be an option, and the potential benefits for modernisation, and for service users and carers, should be a sufficient to spur to action.

Appendix 1: The National Coordinating Centre for Research Capacity Development (NCC RDC)

The NCC RDC is part of a total investment by the Department of Health (DH) of around £40 million in primary care research. The research capacity development programme is a national programme which provides personal awards and funds research infrastructure to support capacity development within the NHS. It is funded by the DH's Research and Development (R&D) programme. The purpose of the programme is to build and support a skilled workforce capable of advancing high-quality research with the aim of maintaining and improving health within a knowledge-based health service. The research capacity development programme works closely with the research community, receiving advice and support through a number of panels and committees.

The aim of the NCC is to ensure that the research priorities and needs of the National Health Service (NHS) can be met by the provision of this research infrastructure and a coordinated programme of training to develop a cadre of researchers sufficient to support those needs. The Centre takes into account the NHS priorities and needs, wider workforce development issues and equity of access to all professions required to deliver the DH and NHS research agenda. Alongside the NCC RCD there are a number of Research and Development Support Units (RDSUs) to promote the research infrastructure. Some of these are beginning to offer small amounts of support within social care.

Personal award schemes

The NHS Research Capacity Development programme currently supports six personal award schemes:

Primary care awards

- Primary care research development awards
- Primary care post-doctoral awards
- Primary care career scientist awards.

Public health career scientist awards

Clinical scientist awards

Nursing and allied health professions awards

- Nursing and allied health professions research (AHP) and development awards
- Nursing and AHP post-doctoral awards.

Complementary and alternative medicine awards (CAM)

- CAM research and development awards
- CAM post-doctoral awards.

Research scientist in evidence (RSES)

- RSES research and development awards
- RSES post-doctoral awards.

In partnership with the Medical Research Council (MRC) the NCC also provides funding to support the joint MRC/DH Health Service Research and Health of the Public special training fellowships. These awards are managed on behalf of the DH by the MRC and in most cases are for doctoral study. In addition, a public health initiative has recently been launched to provide pump-priming funding for public health researchers early in their research careers.

Appendix 2: Breakdown of total public expenditure on health and social services by country

	Health	Social services
England	**£69,369,000,000 (2004-05)** Spending Review 2004-05, Chapter 8, Table 8.1: Key Figures, total NHS (England) www.hm-treasury.gov.uk/media/801/75/sr2004_ch8.pdf	**£10,643,000,000** Spending Review 2004-05, Chapter 8, Table 8.1: Key Figures, total Personal Social Services (England) www.hm-treasury.gov.uk/media/801/75/sr2004_ch8.pdf
Wales	**£4,325,083,000 (2004-05)** National Assembly for Wales Budget 2005-06 to 2007-08, Draft Budget Proposals, 2004-05, Health and Social Services, Original plans www.wales.gov.uk/themesbudgetandstrategic/content/budget2004/budgetplan-e.pdf (sum local health boards and NHS trusts, education and training, family health services, health improvement and health promotion)	**£244,755,000** National Assembly for Wales Budget 2005-06 to 2007-08, Draft budget Proposals, 2004-05, Health and Social Services, original plans www.wales.gov.uk/themesbudgetandstrategic/content/budget2004/budgetplan-e.pdf (sum children, personal social services, other health and social services, social services inspectorate [Wales])
Scotland	**£7,775,660,000 (2004-05)** The Scottish Executive: Draft budget 2004-05 Summary, Chapter 5. Health and community care, Spending plans www.scotland.gov.uk/library5/finance/db05s-07.asp (sum NHS, Health improvement and other health services)	**£230,439,000 (2004-05)** The Scottish Executive: Draft budget 2004-05 Summary, Chapter 5. Health and community care, Spending plans www.scotland.gov.uk/library5/finance/db05s-07.asp (sum community care and mental illness specific grant: £69,190,000), plus Chapter 3, education and young people, Children, young people and social care, Spending Plans 2002-08, Table 3.04 www.scotland.gov.uk/library5/finance/db0506-05.asp (total: £109,705,000)
Northern Ireland	**£2,139,800,000 (2004-05)** The Northern Ireland Draft Priorities and Budget 2005-08, Chapter 6, Departmental Public Service Agreements (PSAs) and proposed budget allocations, Department of Health, Social Services and Public Safety www.pfgbudgetni.gov.uk/draftdocb.pdf (sum hospital, community health [inc discretionary FHS] and Family Health Services)	**£712,600,000 (2004-05)** The Northern Ireland Draft Priorities and Budget 2005-2008, Chapter Six, Departmental Public Service Agreements (PSAs) and Proposed Budget Allocations, Department of Health, Social Services and Public Safety www.pfgbudgetni.gov.uk/draftdocb.pdf (total Personal Social Services)

Note: See Table 2 in the report. (Dr Sheila Fish, SCIE)

Appendix 3: Workforce data

Social care

The major sources of social care workforce data are Skills for care (formerly known as Topss England), the Care Council for Wales, the Northern Ireland Social Care Council and the Scottish Social Services Council. Information is available from their websites and publications. However, two key issues affect the reliability and completeness of this data. First, it is somewhat out of date, often drawn from research conducted in 2001. Second, and more crucially, these figures are far from straightforward and either their comparison or aggregation presents serious problems.

Eborall, in her work for Topss England, stated that "estimating the size and structure of the social care workforce in England presents considerable difficulties, for a wide range of reasons".[59] Most basically, the boundaries of the field itself remain unclear; what types of work are included or not, within which range of services, is a matter of debate. Moreover, within this amorphous grouping, certain sections are still distinctly under-researched. These include the independent sector, people working in domiciliary care, agency workers and those 'casual' workers who are paid in cash. Within data sets that are available, methods of counting vary (headcounts versus full-time equivalents), and this is complicated by the prevalence of part-time working in the field. Similar issues are found in Wales, Scotland and Northern Ireland and different authors address them in different ways. Contacting these bodies directly, requesting information on numbers of qualified social workers and the percentage of these working for local authorities revealed that these limitations are not restricted to published material. Reliable data on various specifics of the social care workforce are simply not yet available.

Social care workforce data

	Total workforce (whole-time equivalent)	Employed by local authorities	Employed by private/independent sector	Gender	Part-time workers	Pay	Turnover	Recruitment/ retention problems	% qualifications	Number of qualified social workers	% of qualified social workers working for local authorities
England	929,000–1,551,000 (median 1,240,000)	284,000 18%–30%	594,000–1,017,000	80%–95% female	Around 50%	Relatively low	Relatively high	Severe	Less than 20% qualified	76,300	69%
Wales	70,000	36% in 'statutory employers'	Private 53% Voluntary 11% Total: 64%	80% female	–	An increase in pay is a common reason for leaving	Recruitment and retention are the two most important factors affecting possibility of a skilled and qualified workforce	Yes	20% have appropriate qualifications	2,768 (figures sent by Ian Thomas, Work Force Development Advisor, Care Council Wales)	About 76.48% (Figures sent by Ian Thomas, Workforce Development Advisor, Care Council Wales)
Scotland	100,000–125,000 (median 112,500)	36%	Private 16% Voluntary 29% Total: 45%	85% female	–	Many are low paid	–	Yes	Only 20% have qualifications	7,000 (Carole Wilkinson, Chief Executive SSSC, personal communication, 25.10.04)	About half (Carole Wilkinson, Chief Executive SSSC, personal communication, 25.10.04)

	Total workforce (whole-time equivalent)	Employed by local authorities	Employed by private/independent sector	Gender	Part-time workers	Pay	Turnover	Recruitment/retention problems	% qualifications	Number of qualified social workers	% of qualified social workers working for local authorities
Northern Ireland	30,000	Approx 30% in statutory sector	70%	Predominantly female	The majority	–	–	Yes	Estimated 80% do not have appropriate qualifications	1,939	Most employed in the statutory and voluntary sector with only a small number in the private sector

Note: See Table 3 in the report.

Sources:
England: Eborall, C. (2003) *The state of the social care workforce in England: Volume 1 of the first Annual Report of the Topss England Workforce Intelligence Unit*, Leeds: Topss (www.topssengland.net/files/vol1%20TopssEnglandwkfce2003re65A.doc).
Wales: Care Council for Wales (2003) *The Skills Foresight Plan for the social care sector in Wales*, Cardiff: CCWales (www.ccwales.org.uk/desktop default.aspx?tabid=130).
Scotland: Scottish Social Services Council (2004) *Fit for the future: Maximising the potential of the social services workforce*, Dundee: SSSC (www.sssc.uk.com/NR/rdonlyres/2EE5C267-737D-4B8B-9E3E-19998D2AD51F/0/SSSCFitfortheFutureA4.pdf).
Northern Ireland: Northern Ireland Social Care Council (2003) *Making a difference: Northern Ireland Social Care Council Corporate Plan 2003-2006*, June (www.niscc.info/about/pdf/Corporate_Plan_2003_2006.pdf).
Northern Ireland Social Care Council (2002) *Workforce planning for social work: Supply, demand and provision of newly qualified social workers required 2001/2-2002/4*. Belfast: NISCC. (www.niscc.info/pdf/wforce_planning_Feb02.pdf) p 8.
Department of Health, Social Services and Public Safety (2003) *Workforce planning review*, November (www.dhsspsni.gov.uk/publications/ahp-docs/Social_Services_Review.pdf)

Health workforce data

The health workforce data are used for comparative purposes in the main body of the report. Health workforce data, in sharp contrast to that in social care, are relatively easily obtainable, with figures for head counts, whole-time equivalents, and key groups of staff fully accessible in the public domain. If more detailed figures, or particular breakdowns, are required then helpful statistics staff are available to provide the details.

The figures below are for 2003, and for totals are whole-time equivalents, allowing comparison with social care. The breakdown of staffing for England provides an overview of the contrast with social care (there is a significantly higher proportion of qualified staff in the NHS), and is provided as a head count.

	Total NHS staff
England	1,027,284
Wales	68,472
Scotland	129,275
Northern Ireland	39,024

NB: qualification not members of staff	Medical qualification	Professionally qualified clinical	Qualifications in nursing, midwifery and health visiting (including practice nurses)	Qualified scientific, therapeutic and technical	Qualified ambulance staff
England	108,000	622,575	386,959	122,066	15,957

	Total primary care practice staff
England	88,424

	Total GPs
England	29,777
Wales	1,780
Scotland	3,921
Northern Ireland	1,002

Note: See Table 3 in the report.

Sources: Staff in the NHS 2003 (DH)

Personal communication: Katie Taylor, Nick Parker, Statistics (Workforce) Division, DH (now Information Centre, NHS)

(Professor Peter Marsh, University of Sheffield)

Appendix 4: Research & Development expenditure

Compiling comparative data on funding for research and development in health and social care respectively also proved to be a difficult task. Public accounting is neither always available nor consistently up to date; figures mentioned are not necessarily referenced or qualified in any way. The Department of Health (DH) manages the National Health Service (NHS) Research and Development (R&D) funding (that replaced the old NHS R&D levy system), for example, providing data on total annual funding allocations. Yet there is no such public annual accounting for its own investment through the Policy Research Programme and the NHS R&D programme. Figures given on the website are unreferenced and unqualified; the database of funded programmes is remarkably out of date, documentation ending 31 December 2000.

Even where accounting is available publicly or on request, the classification of R&D funding does not tend to lend itself to the task generally. The Medical Research Council (MRC) website gives details of funding commitments as totals for the whole life of a research project, specifying that this 'usually spans several years' but giving no further detail. Moreover, the way that R&D funding data are classified is particularly unsuitable for a focus on social care. The Economic and Social Research Council (ESRC) has only recently (2005) recognised social work as a discipline, but its data do not distinguish social work as the 'subject areas' of research projects, seminar programmes, etc. An estimate is that 2.9% of ESRC expenditure applies to social work.[25] The most significant units of assessment used by the Higher Education Funding Councils (HEFCs) in the Research Assessment Exercise (RAE) are social policy and administration and social work. Methods of accounting differ between the funding councils of different countries, further complicating the picture. HEFC England includes 'capability' funding with accounting of Quality-related Research 'QR' allocations, where other countries do not. Even major charities do not tend to differentiate their R&D funding allocations in terms of 'social care'. Consequently, the data provided are far from exact. More details are provided below.

Table A4.1: R&D funding data

	Health	Social Work and social care
Pharm-aceutical industries	**Estimated £2,375,000,000 (1998)** Association of the British Pharmaceutical Industry, www.abpi.org.uk/publications/ briefings/investing.pdf	**No direct equivalent**
NHS levy	**£442,450,561 (2003-04)** DH website, NHS R&D allocations 2004-05 (through the NHS Support for Science and NHS Priorities and Needs R&D funding) www.dh.gov.uk/PolicyAndGuidance/ ResearchAndDevelopment/ ResearchAndDevelopmentAZ/ NationalNHSRDFunding/fs/en NHS allocations 2004-05	**No direct equivalent**
DH	**Approximately £534,700,000 (2002-03)** DH website data on funding through Policy Research programme and the NHS R&D programme, of which 10% is likely to be primary care[60]	**Approximately £5.3 million (1999-2000)** DH website on funding through the Policy Research programme
Research Councils	**MRC: approximately £359.9 million (2003)** 'whole life' cost of awards as of April 2003, £719.9 million, 2 years (SCIE estimate)	**ESRC: £67,482,000 (2003-2004)** Total 'Research expenditure' www.esrc.ac.uk, of which 2.9% is likely to be social work[25]
Major charities	**Approximately £540 million per annum** DH website, combined expenditure including Welcome Trust	**Approximately £10,650,730 (2002-03)** Estimates of relevant funding by the Joseph Rowntree Foundation, Gatsby Trust and Nuffield Foundation – see below
HEFC	**Approximately £233,085,666 (2004-05)** Aggregation of figures for QR funding allocations for clinical laboratory sciences, community-based clinical subjects, hospital-based clinical subjects, nursing and professions allied to medicine, from HEFC England, HEFC Wales, Scottish HEFC and Department of Employment and Learning (DEL) Northern Ireland – see detailed tables below	**Approximately £18,944,125 (2004-05)** Aggregation of figures for QR Funding allocations for social policy and administration and social work from HEFC England, HEFC Wales, Scottish HEFC andDepartment of Employment and Learning (DEL) Northern Ireland – see detailed tables below.

Breakdown of HEFCs' (or equivalent) allocation of mainstream QR funds for selected units of assessment grant allocations

Table A4.2: HEFCE (Higher Education Funding Council for England)
(including funds for London Extra Costs, PGR supervision; 2003-04 figures include transitional funding for students in '3b' rated departments and supplement for 5* in 1996-2001; 2004-05 include funds for 'the best 5*' departments, funds for 'the best 5*' departments plus supplement, where appropriate, to maintain funds at the 2003-04 level)

Unit of assessment	2002-03 research funding mainstream QR (£)	2003-04 research funding mainstream QR (£)	2004-05 research funding mainstream QR and capability (£)
Clinical laboratory sciences	34,674,845	39,624,486	43,349,578
Community-based clinical subjects	27,196,850	31,005,876	33,991,694
Hospital-based clinical subjects	78,621,161	90,417,791	96,105,599
Nursing	6,048,737	5,477,048	5,415,020
Professions allied to medicine	19,674,413	18,557,179	19,834,452
Total	**116,216,006**	**185,082,380**	**198, 696,344**
Social policy and administration	12,350,641	11,893,613	12,059,642
Social work	3,689,912	3,313,262	3,319,961
Total	**16,040,554**	**15,206,875**	**15,379,603**

Source: www.hefce.ac.uk/research/funding/QRFunding/

Table A4.3: HEFCW (Higher Education Funding Council for Wales)

Unit of assessment	2003-04 total QR allocations
Clinical laboratory sciences	£1,505,338
Community-based clinical subjects	£1,238,888
Hospital-based clinical subjects	£2,037,896
Nursing	£1,083,453
Professions allied to medicine	£1,906,807
Social policy and administration	£661,415
Social work	£344,811

Source: HEFCW 'Higher Education Funding Council for Wales Funding Allocations 2003/2004'

Table A4.4: SHEFC (Scottish Higher Education Funding Council)

Unit of assessment	Total main QR grant allocation 2003-04	Total main QR grant allocation 2004-05
Clinical laboratory sciences	5,045,214	5,708,912
Community-based clinical subjects	2,794,894	2,970,371
Hospital-based clinical subjects	7,122,205	8,197,901
Nursing	114,652	119,307
Professions allied to medicine	1,753,150	1,867,090
Social policy and administration	739,089	765,643
Social work	896,761	996,609

Source: 2003-04 www.shefc.ac.uk/library, Table B2
2004-05 www.shefc.ac.uk/library, Table_B2.xls

Table A4.5: Department of Employment and Learning (DEL) Northern Ireland[*]

Unit of assessment	Main QR grant to each unit of allocation (subject) 2003-04	Main QR grant to each unit of allocation (subject) 2004-05
Clinical laboratory sciences	1,359,602	1,450,758
Community-based clinical subjects	479,415	530,497
Hospital-based clinical subjects	826,317	788,971
Nursing	533,677	518,939
Professions allied to medicine	4,184,723	4,464,194
Social policy and administration	567,343	581,960
Social work	219,707	214,083

Source: Data provided by Marty Fullerton, Higher Education Research Policy Branch, DEL

---

[*] DEL is that body that distributes research funding, taking advice from the Northern Ireland Higher Education Council.

Breakdown of major charities R&D funding for social work and social care

Joseph Rowntree Foundation	**£390,169 (2003)** Estimate of social care related projects from 'Projects of over £15,000 supported by the Joseph Rowntree Foundation in 2003' www.jrf.org.uk/about/pdf/projects2003.pdf
The Gatsby Charitable Foundation	**£7,841,561 (2002-03)** Estimate based on the total sum of the two fields of activities funded that are most related to social care: mental health total grant payments 2002-03, £2,619,812 Disadvantaged children total grant payments 2002-03, £5,221,749 www.gatsby.org.uk/80256C6900379063/WebLaunch/LaunchMe
Nuffield Foundation	**£2,419,000 (2003)** Sum of grants awarded through the 'Social Research and Innovation' programme for the year ending December 2003 www.nuffieldfoundation.org/fileLibrary/pdf/Nuffield_annual_accounts_2003.pdf

Note: See Table 4 in the report.

Appendix 5: Priorities for knowledge development

The main section of this report calls attention to the way that, in the area of primary care, a far-reaching inquiry – known as the Mant Report[16] – created the infrastructure for serious and sustained knowledge development to support evidence-based policy and practice. In order to achieve this scale of reform in the infrastructure to support knowledge production in social care, we have called for an equivalent of the Mant Report to be commissioned.

Such an inquiry would undoubtedly need to explore the investment and resources required to modernise evidence production for the social care sector. However, it would also need to highlight some of the priorities that such investment and resources might be used to explore. This appendix outlines a number of immediate priorities for knowledge development.

Methodological development

Social problems and issues typically have multiple causes and this means that the infrastructure for social care knowledge production will require a variety of methodological approaches. Social care research increasingly demands an interdisciplinary team perspective and this will also bring the need to integrate different methodological approaches. The field is further characterised by a high commitment to participatory and emancipatory approaches, and social care research requires the sophisticated development of ways of involving those who use social care and those who deliver it.

The field has traditionally suffered unhelpful 'paradigm wars' between quantitative and qualitative methods. Fortunately, significant progress was made on this issue during the *Theorising Social Work Research Seminar Series* in 2000, which produced a broad view of methodology that merits widespread support (see papers at www.scie.org.uk/publications/misc/tswr/index.asp). In particular, Joyce Lishman showed the futility of traditional 'paradigm wars', and validated a number of approaches to what constitutes scientific evidence, including participative, or empowering research that engages service users' and carers' knowledge and skills[61]. Nick Gould underlined the necessity for multi-method approaches underpinned by theoretical pluralism[62]. In revisiting his critique of naïve positivism, David Smith reiterated the limitations of single-method approaches underpinning one version of evidence-based practice, and alerts us to the simplistic liaison between positivist researchers seeking law-like generalisations, and managers and politicians seeking definitive solutions to social problems. In supporting realist approaches, Smith[63,64] suggests that:

> ... rather than trying to replicate programmes which seem to work in the hope that they will work everywhere and always, we should try to generalise about programmes by developing middle-range theories about context-mechanism-outcome patterns which will allow us to interpret differences and similarities among groups of programmes. This is the realist alternative to the aspirations of the experimental method of positivism, which, hypnotised by method to the point where theory is forgotten, has rarely managed to tell us anything helpful

about the questions that matter: what is it about this programme that works for whom in what specifiable conditions and given what contextual features.[63]

The seminar series provides a rationale for rejecting single-method approaches and for choosing methodological diversity. However, two main dangers remain. First, the sheer popularity among managers and politicians of the 'what works' slogan will count against the more realistic, but more cautious 'what works with whom, according to whose definition, and under what conditions'. The pressure for methodological diversity risks being seen as holding back the evidence-based modernisation of social care. This means that the voices of methodological diversity must be heard at the national level in debates about evidence-based policy and practice, and the long-term value of the careful accumulation of sophisticated bodies of evidence must be emphasised.

A second danger is that we risk confusing principled, methodological pluralism with random eclecticism. Knowledge production in social work and social care has a sad history of the unprincipled adoption of methods and it is partly this weakness that provides the fertile ground for narrowly defined methodological schools. If methodological pluralism is to form part of the strategic infrastructure, therefore, the research community will need increasing sophistication in its choice and rationale for multi-method approaches.

The current prospect for this is bright. The Social Care Institute for Excellence (SCIE) has developed a standpoint on including diverse types of knowledge in its reviews of the evidence base, assisted by the Economic and Social Research Council (ESRC)-funded EvidenceNetwork, a group of research centres lead by Professor Ken Young at Queen Mary, University of London (see www.evidencenetwork.org and).[14] This inclusive perspective on the kinds of relevant knowledge provides a clear foundation for a similarly inclusive approach to the methods of producing knowledge.

As the major national resource for the development of methods of social research, the ESRC has also invested in a new national methods centre (www.ncrm.ac.uk) and continuing development from this centre will be required. The ESRC has also recently recognised social work as an academic discipline under which research proposals may be made[25] and now publishes research training requirements specific to social work.

These developments bring the possibility of strong social science support for the development of specific research methods appropriate to social work and social care.

Knowledge use

Within social work and social care, there are long-standing debates about the nature of social work knowledge and about the relationship between research-based knowledge and practice. Best practice in social care is increasingly subject to guidance from SCIE, whose brief includes defining quality services, working across existing sectors, and developing implementation strategies to spread good practice and to support change.

All this points to the urgent need to prioritise work on the acquisition and adoption of knowledge for practice. In the healthcare field, a recent systematic review proposed new ways of conceptualising the use of research-based evidence, and points to the need for further work to identify what levels of knowledge are required for which tasks, how different members of the workforce learn, how best to ensure knowledge transfer and implementation, and how to ensure durability of impact.[65]

In social care, SCIE has recently published a review of approaches to research use that explores three models – the research-based practitioner, the embedded research model and the organisational excellence model – and that makes clear the case for examining the way the system as a whole operates to encourage or impede research use in practice.[66]

Much of the existing approach, however, is based on the assumption that research-based knowledge is produced outside social care practice, and then applied in a linear fashion. A strategic approach to infrastructure development would also require the recognition that practice itself is a key source of knowledge[67] and that such knowledge-use-in-practice is a key area for research.[68]

What is required is substantial investment in a programme of work to build cumulative and sophisticated knowledge about how practitioners use knowledge in practice, a programme that would necessarily be multi-disciplinary[44] and that would generate a debate both about how practice can identify issues for the research agenda, and how research-based knowledge can be integrated with the knowledge practitioners already use.

Systematic reviews

Systematic reviews are now recognised as an essential tool in evidence-based policy and practice, allowing the weaknesses of individual studies to be set in the context of a body of work that is synthesised to yield more reliable and valid messages. Systematic reviews also serve to highlight gaps in knowledge.

Unlike healthcare, social work and social care has a relatively under-developed capacity to undertake systematic reviews, with no national centre and no training programme to increase the numbers of review and development (R&D) personnel able to conduct reviews. The Campbell Collaboration (C2), intended as a sister to the Cochrane Collaboration, has a subgroup covering social welfare, and methods groups addressing the protocols for systematic reviews. The social welfare group is unsupported by any funding body or by central government, and thus lacks infrastructure and continuity, which in turn hampers the development of a register of protocols and reviews and of an appropriately qualified editorial group.

If systematic reviews are to become a critical tool in evidence-based policy and practice, longer-term investment in capacity building is required. This calls for the kind of training and educational work undertaken by the Cochrane Collaboration, but also for specific attention to issues such as user and carer involvement in systematic reviews and to methods of narrative synthesis (to apply equally rigorous methods to the synthesis of non-quantitative data as are applied to quantitative data).

Human resource management (HRM)

The UK social care workforce is estimated at 1.4 million, with one third employed by local authorities and two thirds employed by an estimated 25,000 or more private and independent agencies (see Appendix 3). It is a predominantly female workforce, with relatively low pay and high turnover. About 80% have no qualifications whatsoever. Only 86,000 are qualified social workers, of whom almost 70% are employed in local authorities. There are severe recruitment and retention problems, particularly in the South East.

There is only one, relatively small, specialist Social Care Workforce Research Unit, located at Kings College London. Mainstream employment research in the UK has largely ignored this workforce, with the consequence that we lack an evidence base for key HRM strategies. In particular, we know very little about the contribution HRM can make to the central government quality agenda: for example, we do not know, in social care, whether specific HRM practices can influence recruitment and retention, increase the occupational or organisational commitment of staff, or influence the quality of front-line performance.

Thus, the 'quality' agenda will continue to be limited in its evidence base unless the infrastructure for social care R&D includes focused attention on workforce issues.

Summary

The priorities outlined here are relatively general: they do not focus on issues specific to any particular group of service users, for example, or on particular social care interventions. They may seem rather abstract to the policy maker, who will be used, in the healthcare arena, to more specific detail deriving from agreed, national priorities (such as cancer care). They may seem equally abstract to practitioners and researchers, who will have pressing concerns deriving from immediate service requirements or from existing research studies. These priorities may thus seem to have few friends.

In a sense, it is precisely this gap that this report has tried to highlight – the key infrastructure issues that no one specifically owns or has a brief to develop, and yet which must be addressed if evidence-based policy and practice is to be successful in social care.

References

1   Editorial (2003) 'Is primary care research a lost cause?', *The Lancet*, vol 361, p 977.

2   Fisher, M. and Marsh, P. (2003) 'Social work research and the 2001 Research Assessment Exercise: an initial overview', *Social Work Education*, vol 22, no 1, pp 71-80.

3   Davies, H.T.O., Nutley, S.M. and Smith, P.C. (eds) (2000) *What works? Evidence-based policy and practice in public services*, Bristol: The Policy Press.

4   Trinder, L. (2000) 'Evidence-based practice in social work and probation', in L. Trinder and S. Reynolds (eds) *Evidence-based Practice: A critical appraisal*, Oxford: Blackwell Science, pp 138-162.

5   Mulgan, G. (2005) 'Government, knowledge and the business of policy making: the potential and limits of evidence-based policy', *Evidence & Policy: A Journal of Research, Debate and Practice*, vol 1, no 2, pp 215-226.

6   Marsh, P. (in press) 'Promoting children's welfare by interprofessional practice and learning in social work and primary care', *Social Work Education*.

7   Duncan, S. (2005) 'Changing social scene', *Horizons (National Statistics)*, no 32, pp 26-27.

8   Davies, P. (2004) 'Systematic reviews and the Campbell Collaboration', in S. Thomas (ed) *Evidence-based practice in education*, Buckingham: Open University Press, pp 21-33.

9   Davies, P. and Boruch, R. (2001) 'The Campbell Collaboration: does for public policy what Cochrane does for health', *British Medical Journal*, no 323, pp 294-295.

10 Department of Health (2005) *Best research for best health: A new national health research strategy*, London: Department of Health.

11 Tierney, L. (1993) 'Practice research and social work education', *Australian Social Work*, vol 46, no 2, pp 9-22.

12 Lewis, J. (2001) 'What works in community care?', *Managing Community Care*, vol 9, no 1, pp 3-6.

13 Beresford, P. (2003) *It's our lives: A short theory of knowledge, distance and experience*, London: The Citizen's Press.

14 Pawson, R., Boaz, A., Grayson, L., Long, A. and Barnes, C. (2003) *Types and quality of knowledge in social care*, London: Social Care Institute for Excellence.

15   Gambrill, E. (1999) 'Evidence-based practice: an alternative to authority-based practice', *Families in Society: The Journal of Contemporary Human Services*, vol 80, no 4, pp 341-350.

16   Department of Health (1997) *R&D in primary care*, London: The Stationery Office.

17   Department of Health (1994) *A wider strategy for research and development relating to personal social services*, London: The Stationery Office.

18   CCETSW (Central Council for Education and Training in Social Work) and PSSC (Personal Social Services Council) (1980) *Research and practice: Report of a Working Party on a research strategy for the personal social services*, London: CCETSW and PSSC.

19   Statham, J. (1992) *Survey of resources for research relevant to the personal social services*, London: Thomas Coram Research Unit.

20   Department of Health (1992) *Review of the role of DH-funded research units: Report to the Director of Research and Development*, London: Department of Health.

21   Lewis, J. and Ritchie, J. (1995) *Advancing research: Research workforce capacity in health and social care*, London: Social and Community Planning Research.

22   Department of Health (1992) *Research capacity strategy for the Department of Health and the NHS*, London: Department of Health.

23   Department of Health and Social Security (1985) *Social work decisions in child care*, London: HMSO.

24   Department of Health (1991) *Patterns and outcomes in child placement*, London: HMSO.

25   Shaw, I., Arksey, H., and Mullender, A. (2004) *ESRC research, social work and social care*, London: Social Care Institute for Excellence.

26   Department of Health (1996) *Primary care: Delivering the future*, London: The Stationery Office.

27   MRC (Medical Research Council) (1997) *Primary health care (topic review)*, London: MRC.

28   Society of Academic Primary Care (2002) *New Century, new challenges*, London: Royal College of General Practitioners.

29   Gibbons, M., Limoges, C., Nowotny, H., Schwartzmann, S., Scott, P. and Trow, M. (1994) *The new production of knowledge: The dynamics of science and research in contemporary societies*, London: Sage Publications.

30 Fisher, M. (1999) 'Social work research, social work knowledge and the Research Assessment Exercise', in R. Broad (ed) *The politics of social work research*, Birmingham: Venture Press, pp 91-108.

31 Philp, M. (1979) 'Notes on the form of knowledge in social work', *Sociological Review*, vol 27, no 1, pp 83-111.

32 Barnes, M. (1992) 'Research and user involvement: contributions to learning and methods', in M. Barnes and G. Wistow G. (eds) *Researching user involvement*, Leeds: The Nuffield Institute, pp 86-105.

33 Beresford, P. and Campbell, J. (1994) 'Disabled people, service users, user involvement and representation', *Disability and Society*, vol 9, no 3, pp 315-325.

34 Lindow, V. and Morris, J. (1995) *Service User involvement: Synthesis of findings and experience in the field of community care*, York: Joseph Rowntree Foundation.

35 Carr, S. (2004) *Has service user participation made a difference to social care services?*, London: Social Care Institute for Excellence.

36 Butler, I. (2003) 'Doing good research and doing it well: ethical awareness and the production of social work research', *Social Work Education*, vol 22, no 1, pp 19-30.

37 Fisher, M. (2002) 'The role of service users in problem formulation and technical aspects of social research', *Social Work Education*, vol 21, no 3, pp 305-312.

38 Sheldon, B. and Chilvers, R. (2001) *Evidence-based social care: Problems and prospects*, Lyme Regis: Russell House.

39 Shaw, I. (1999) *Qualitative evaluation*, London: Sage Publications.

40 McCartt-Hess, P. and Mullen, E. (1995) 'Bridging the gap: collaborative considerations in practitioner-researcher knowledge-building partnerships', in P. McCartt-Hess and E. Mullen (eds) Practitioner-researcher partnerships: Building knowledge from, in and for practice, Washington DC: NASW Press, pp 1-30.

41 Gambrill, E. (1990) *Critical thinking in clinical practice*, San Francisco, CA: Jossey-Bass.

42 Nurius, P., Kemp, S. and Gibson, J. (1999) 'Practitioners' perspectives on sound reasoning: adding a worker-in-context perspective', *Administration in Social Work*, vol 23, no 1, pp 1-27.

43 Sheppard, M., Newstead, S., DiCaccavo, A., and Ryan, K. (2000) 'Reflexivity and the development of process knowledge in social work: a classification and empirical study', *British Journal of Social Work*, vol 30, no 4, pp 465-488.

44   Sheppard, M., Newstead, S., DiCaccavo, A. and Ryan, K. (2001) 'Comparative hypothesis assessment, triangulation and quasi triangulation as process knowledge assessment strategies in social work practice', *British Journal of Social Work*, vol 31, no 6, pp 863-885.

45   Fook, J. (1996) *The reflective researcher: Social workers' theories of practice research*, London: Allen and Unwin.

46   Fook, J., Ryan, M., and Hawkins, L. (1997) 'Towards a theory of social work expertise', *British Journal of Social Work*, vol 27, pp 399-417.

47   Fook, J. (2000) 'Critical perspective on social work practice', in I. O'Connor, J. Warburton and P. Smythe (eds) *Contemporary perspectives on social work and the human services: Challenges and change*, Melbourne: Addison Wesley Longman, pp 129-138.

48   Proctor, E. and Rosen, A. (2000) 'The structure and function of social work practice guidelines', Paper prepared for *Toward the development of practice guidelines for social work intervention*, St Louis, MS: George Warren Brown School of Social Work, Washington University, 3-5 May.

49   Jarvis, P. and Gibson, S. (1997) *The teacher practitioner and mentor*, Cheltenham: Stanley Thornes.

50   Department of Health (1999) *Making a difference: Strengthening the nursing, midwifery and health visiting contribution to health care*, London: Department of Health.

51   Redwood, S., Childs, J., Burrows, M., Aylott, M. and Andrews, C. (2002) *Beyond closing the gap: An evaluation of the lecturer-practitioner role*, Bournemouth: Institute of Health and Community Studies, Bournemouth University.

52   Goodlad, S. (ed) (1984) *Education for the professions*, Guildford: Society for Research into Higher Education and National Forum for Education Research.

53   Barnett, R., Becher, R.A. and Cork, N.M. (1987) 'Models of professional preparation: pharmacy, nursing and teaching education', *Studies in Higher Education*, vol 12, pp 51-63.

54   Taylor, I. (1997) *Developing learning and professional education*, Buckingham: Open University Press.

55   Fairbrother, P. and Mathers, N.J. (2004) 'Combining cultures: lecturer-practitioners in six professions', *Journal of Clinical Nursing*, vol 13, pp 539-546.

56   Morris, A. (2005) 'Evidence initiatives: aspects of recent experience in England', *Evidence & Policy: A Journal of Research, Debate and Practice*, vol 1, no 2, pp 257-268.

57 Smith, H., Owen, J., Marsh, P. and Cooke, J. (2001) *Developing research at the social services and health interface: A study for the Trent Focus Group*: Sheffield: University of Sheffield Children and Families Welfare Research Programme and Trent Focus Group.

58 StLaR (Strategic Learning and Research Committee) (2004) *Developing and sustaining a world class workforce of educators and researchers in health and social care*, London: Department for Education and Skills, Department of Health and NHS University.

59 Eborall, C. (2003) *The State of the social care workforce in England: Volume 1 of the First Annual Report of the Topss England Workforce Intelligence Unit*, Leeds: TOPSS.

60 Campbell, S.M., Roland, M.O., Bentley, E., Dowell, J., Hassall, K., Pooley, J.E. and Price, H. (1999) 'Research capacity in UK primary care', *British Journal of General Practice*, vol 49, pp 967-970.

61 Lishman, J. (2000) 'Evidence for practice: the contribution of competing research methodologies' (available at www.scie.org.uk/publications/misc/tswr/seminar5.asp).

62 Gould, N. (2000) 'Qualitative research and the development of best attainable knowledge in social work' (available at www.scie.org.uk/publications/misc/tswr/seminar5.asp).

63 Smith, D. (2000) 'The limits of positivism revisited' (available at www.scie.org.uk/publications/misc/tswr/seminar5.asp)

64 Smith, D. (2004) 'Introduction: some versions of evidence-based practice', in D. Smith (ed) *Social work and evidence-based practice*, London: Jessica Kingsley, pp 7-27.

65 Freemantle, N., Wood, J. and Mason, J. (1999) *Evaluating change in professional behaviour: Issues in design and analysis*, York: Centre for Health Economics, University of York.

66 Nutley, S., Walter, I., Percy-Smith, J., McNeish, D. and Frost, S. (2004) *Improving the Use of research in social care practice*, London: Social Care Institute for Excellence.

67 Kondrat, M.E. (1992) 'Reclaiming the practical: formal and substantive rationality in social work practice', *Social Service Review*, vol 66, pp 237-255.

68 Osmond, J. and O'Connor, I. (2004) 'Formalizing the unformalized: practitioners' communication of knowledge in practice', *British Journal of Social Work*, vol 34, pp 677-692.